C-4168 CAREER EXAMINATION SERIES

This is your
PASSBOOK for...

Esthetician

Test Preparation Study Guide
Questions & Answers

NATIONAL LEARNING CORPORATION®

COPYRIGHT NOTICE

This book is SOLELY intended for, is sold ONLY to, and its use is RESTRICTED to individual, bona fide applicants or candidates who qualify by virtue of having seriously filed applications for appropriate license, certificate, professional and/or promotional advancement, higher school matriculation, scholarship, or other legitimate requirements of education and/or governmental authorities.

This book is NOT intended for use, class instruction, tutoring, training, duplication, copying, reprinting, excerption, or adaptation, etc., by:

1) Other publishers
2) Proprietors and/or Instructors of "Coaching" and/or Preparatory Courses
3) Personnel and/or Training Divisions of commercial, industrial, and governmental organizations
4) Schools, colleges, or universities and/or their departments and staffs, including teachers and other personnel
5) Testing Agencies or Bureaus
6) Study groups which seek by the purchase of a single volume to copy and/or duplicate and/or adapt this material for use by the group as a whole without having purchased individual volumes for each of the members of the group
7) Et al.

Such persons would be in violation of appropriate Federal and State statutes.

PROVISION OF LICENSING AGREEMENTS – Recognized educational, commercial, industrial, and governmental institutions and organizations, and others legitimately engaged in educational pursuits, including training, testing, and measurement activities, may address request for a licensing agreement to the copyright owners, who will determine whether, and under what conditions, including fees and charges, the materials in this book may be used them. In other words, a licensing facility exists for the legitimate use of the material in this book on other than an individual basis. However, it is asseverated and affirmed here that the material in this book CANNOT be used without the receipt of the express permission of such a licensing agreement from the Publishers. Inquiries re licensing should be addressed to the company, attention rights and permissions department.

All rights reserved, including the right of reproduction in whole or in part, in any form or by any means, electronic or mechanical, including photocopying, recording, or by any information storage and retrieval system, without permission in writing from the Publisher.

Copyright © 2025 by
National Learning Corporation

212 Michael Drive, Syosset, NY 11791
(516) 921-8888 • www.passbooks.com
E-mail: info@passbooks.com

PASSBOOK® SERIES

THE *PASSBOOK® SERIES* has been created to prepare applicants and candidates for the ultimate academic battlefield – the examination room.

At some time in our lives, each and every one of us may be required to take an examination – for validation, matriculation, admission, qualification, registration, certification, or licensure.

Based on the assumption that every applicant or candidate has met the basic formal educational standards, has taken the required number of courses, and read the necessary texts, the *PASSBOOK® SERIES* furnishes the one special preparation which may assure passing with confidence, instead of failing with insecurity. Examination questions – together with answers – are furnished as the basic vehicle for study so that the mysteries of the examination and its compounding difficulties may be eliminated or diminished by a sure method.

This book is meant to help you pass your examination provided that you qualify and are serious in your objective.

The entire field is reviewed through the huge store of content information which is succinctly presented through a provocative and challenging approach – the question-and-answer method.

A climate of success is established by furnishing the correct answers at the end of each test.

You soon learn to recognize types of questions, forms of questions, and patterns of questioning. You may even begin to anticipate expected outcomes.

You perceive that many questions are repeated or adapted so that you can gain acute insights, which may enable you to score many sure points.

You learn how to confront new questions, or types of questions, and to attack them confidently and work out the correct answers.

You note objectives and emphases, and recognize pitfalls and dangers, so that you may make positive educational adjustments.

Moreover, you are kept fully informed in relation to new concepts, methods, practices, and directions in the field.

You discover that you are actually taking the examination all the time: you are preparing for the examination by "taking" an examination, not by reading extraneous and/or supererogatory textbooks.

In short, this PASSBOOK®, used directedly, should be an important factor in helping you to pass your test.

ESTHETICIAN

SCOPE OF THE WRITTEN TEST

SCIENTIFIC CONCEPTS 60%
Sanitation and Infection Control
- Microbiology
  - Pathogenic & nonpathogenic bacteria
  - Viruses
  - Animal and plant parasites (e.g., lice, fungi)
- Levels of infection control
  - Sanitation
  - Disinfection
  - Sterilization
- Methods of infection control
- Safety procedures
  - OSHA blood borne pathogen standards
  - Material Safety Data Sheets
  - (MSDS)
  - Blood spill procedures

Human Physiology and Anatomy
- Cells
  - Structure
  - Growth & reproduction
- Tissues
- Organs
- Systems and their functions
  - Skeletal
  - Muscular
  - Nervous
  - Vascular/circulatory

Integumentary System and Skin Histology
- Structure and function of the layers of the skin

ESTHETICS PRACTICES 40%
Skin Analysis and Implementation Procedures related to Consultation, Documentation, and Treatment
- Client consultation
- Draping
- Skin analysis
  - Skin types
  - Fitzpatrick Scale
- Treatment protocol
- and contraindications
- Documentation

Product Application and Removal Procedures

- Epidermis
- Dermis
- Subcutaneous
- Glands
  - Sebaceous
  - Sudoriferous
- Functions of the skin
  - Protection
  - Sensation
  - Temperature regulation
  - Excretion
  - Secretion
  - Absorption

Disorders of the Sebaceous and Sudoriferous Glands
Skin Conditions, Disorders, and Diseases
- Inflammation and rashes
- Pigmentation
- Skin growths and lesions

Hair, Follicle, and its Growth Cycle
Basic Chemistry
- Acidity/Alkalinity (pH)
- Organic and Inorganic

Skin Care Products
- Ingredients
- Composition

Factors that Affect the Skin
- Intrinsic factors
- Extrinsic factors

Cleansing Procedures
Steaming Procedures
Exfoliation Procedures
- Chemical
- Physical

Extraction Procedures

Massage Manipulations and Their Effects
- Effleurage
- Petrissage
- Friction
- Tapotement
- Vibration
- Dr. Jacquet

Appropriate Use for Masks
Electricity and Use of Electrical
Devices
Hair Removal Procedures
Color Theory and Makeup Application

General Knowledge of Specialized Services
- Face and body treatments (e.g., body wraps, aromatherapy, body scrubs, lymphatic drainage, reflexology, camouflage makeup, hydrotherapy)
- Terminology related to cosmetic procedures

SAMPLE QUESTIONS

The following sample questions are similar to those on the written examination. Each question is followed by four answer choices. Only one choice is correct. Correct answers are listed following the sample questions.

1. What is the term for the scientific study of the skin?
    A. Myology
    B. Angiology
    C. Physiology
    D. Dermatology

2. A product containing antiseptic reaches what level of decontamination?
    A. Disinfection
    B. Sterilization
    C. Ionization
    D. Sanitation

3. Which of the following is also referred to as the basal layer?
    A. Stratum granulosum
    B. Stratum tucidum
    C. Stratum germinativum
    D. Stratum corneum

4. During the anagen phase of hair growth, the hair
    A. beginning to destroy itself.
    B. actively growing.
    C. shedding.
    D. disconnecting from the papilla.

5. A new client schedules for a series of chemical exfoliation treatments. When should the consultation form be reviewed and signed?
    A. Monthly
    B. Annually
    C. At the first treatment
    D. At each treatment

6. Dilated capillaries that can be seen beneath the surface of the skin are known as
    A. seborrhea.
    B. keratoma.
    C. tetangectasia.
    D. dehydrated.

7. Melanocytes that are more active will produce
    A. lighter skin.
    B. darker skin.
    C. sebaceous skin.
    D. dry skin.

8. In addition to softening sebum, another function of a facial steamer is to
    A. oxygenate the skin.
    B. moisturize the skin.
    C. decrease circulation.
    D. detoxify the skin.

KEY (CORRECT ANSWERS) 1. D, 2. D, 3. C, 4. B, 5. D, 6. C, 7. B, 8. A

HOW TO TAKE A TEST

I. YOU MUST PASS AN EXAMINATION

A. *WHAT EVERY CANDIDATE SHOULD KNOW*

Examination applicants often ask us for help in preparing for the written test. What can I study in advance? What kinds of questions will be asked? How will the test be given? How will the papers be graded?

As an applicant for a civil service examination, you may be wondering about some of these things. Our purpose here is to suggest effective methods of advance study and to describe civil service examinations.

Your chances for success on this examination can be increased if you know how to prepare. Those "pre-examination jitters" can be reduced if you know what to expect. You can even experience an adventure in good citizenship if you know why civil service exams are given.

B. *WHY ARE CIVIL SERVICE EXAMINATIONS GIVEN?*

Civil service examinations are important to you in two ways. As a citizen, you want public jobs filled by employees who know how to do their work. As a job seeker, you want a fair chance to compete for that job on an equal footing with other candidates. The best-known means of accomplishing this two-fold goal is the competitive examination.

Exams are widely publicized throughout the nation. They may be administered for jobs in federal, state, city, municipal, town or village governments or agencies.

Any citizen may apply, with some limitations, such as the age or residence of applicants. Your experience and education may be reviewed to see whether you meet the requirements for the particular examination. When these requirements exist, they are reasonable and applied consistently to all applicants. Thus, a competitive examination may cause you some uneasiness now, but it is your privilege and safeguard.

C. *HOW ARE CIVIL SERVICE EXAMS DEVELOPED?*

Examinations are carefully written by trained technicians who are specialists in the field known as "psychological measurement," in consultation with recognized authorities in the field of work that the test will cover. These experts recommend the subject matter areas or skills to be tested; only those knowledges or skills important to your success on the job are included. The most reliable books and source materials available are used as references. Together, the experts and technicians judge the difficulty level of the questions.

Test technicians know how to phrase questions so that the problem is clearly stated. Their ethics do not permit "trick" or "catch" questions. Questions may have been tried out on sample groups, or subjected to statistical analysis, to determine their usefulness.

Written tests are often used in combination with performance tests, ratings of training and experience, and oral interviews. All of these measures combine to form the best-known means of finding the right person for the right job.

II. HOW TO PASS THE WRITTEN TEST

A. NATURE OF THE EXAMINATION

To prepare intelligently for civil service examinations, you should know how they differ from school examinations you have taken. In school you were assigned certain definite pages to read or subjects to cover. The examination questions were quite detailed and usually emphasized memory. Civil service exams, on the other hand, try to discover your present ability to perform the duties of a position, plus your potentiality to learn these duties. In other words, a civil service exam attempts to predict how successful you will be. Questions cover such a broad area that they cannot be as minute and detailed as school exam questions.

In the public service similar kinds of work, or positions, are grouped together in one "class." This process is known as *position-classification*. All the positions in a class are paid according to the salary range for that class. One class title covers all of these positions, and they are all tested by the same examination.

B. FOUR BASIC STEPS

1) Study the announcement

How, then, can you know what subjects to study? Our best answer is: "Learn as much as possible about the class of positions for which you've applied." The exam will test the knowledge, skills and abilities needed to do the work.

Your most valuable source of information about the position you want is the official exam announcement. This announcement lists the training and experience qualifications. Check these standards and apply only if you come reasonably close to meeting them.

The brief description of the position in the examination announcement offers some clues to the subjects which will be tested. Think about the job itself. Review the duties in your mind. Can you perform them, or are there some in which you are rusty? Fill in the blank spots in your preparation.

Many jurisdictions preview the written test in the exam announcement by including a section called "Knowledge and Abilities Required," "Scope of the Examination," or some similar heading. Here you will find out specifically what fields will be tested.

2) Review your own background

Once you learn in general what the position is all about, and what you need to know to do the work, ask yourself which subjects you already know fairly well and which need improvement. You may wonder whether to concentrate on improving your strong areas or on building some background in your fields of weakness. When the announcement has specified "some knowledge" or "considerable knowledge," or has used adjectives like "beginning principles of..." or "advanced ... methods," you can get a clue as to the number and difficulty of questions to be asked in any given field. More questions, and hence broader coverage, would be included for those subjects which are more important in the work. Now weigh your strengths and weaknesses against the job requirements and prepare accordingly.

3) Determine the level of the position

Another way to tell how intensively you should prepare is to understand the level of the job for which you are applying. Is it the entering level? In other words, is this the position in which beginners in a field of work are hired? Or is it an intermediate or advanced level? Sometimes this is indicated by such words as "Junior" or "Senior" in the class title. Other jurisdictions use Roman numerals to designate the level – Clerk I, Clerk II, for example. The word "Supervisor" sometimes appears in the title. If the level is not indicated by the title, check the description of duties. Will you be working under very close supervision, or will you have responsibility for independent decisions in this work?

4) Choose appropriate study materials

Now that you know the subjects to be examined and the relative amount of each subject to be covered, you can choose suitable study materials. For beginning level jobs, or even advanced ones, if you have a pronounced weakness in some aspect of your training, read a modern, standard textbook in that field. Be sure it is up to date and has general coverage. Such books are normally available at your library, and the librarian will be glad to help you locate one. For entry-level positions, questions of appropriate difficulty are chosen – neither highly advanced questions, nor those too simple. Such questions require careful thought but not advanced training.

If the position for which you are applying is technical or advanced, you will read more advanced, specialized material. If you are already familiar with the basic principles of your field, elementary textbooks would waste your time. Concentrate on advanced textbooks and technical periodicals. Think through the concepts and review difficult problems in your field.

These are all general sources. You can get more ideas on your own initiative, following these leads. For example, training manuals and publications of the government agency which employs workers in your field can be useful, particularly for technical and professional positions. A letter or visit to the government department involved may result in more specific study suggestions, and certainly will provide you with a more definite idea of the exact nature of the position you are seeking.

III. KINDS OF TESTS

Tests are used for purposes other than measuring knowledge and ability to perform specified duties. For some positions, it is equally important to test ability to make adjustments to new situations or to profit from training. In others, basic mental abilities not dependent on information are essential. Questions which test these things may not appear as pertinent to the duties of the position as those which test for knowledge and information. Yet they are often highly important parts of a fair examination. For very general questions, it is almost impossible to help you direct your study efforts. What we can do is to point out some of the more common of these general abilities needed in public service positions and describe some typical questions.

1) General information

Broad, general information has been found useful for predicting job success in some kinds of work. This is tested in a variety of ways, from vocabulary lists to questions about current events. Basic background in some field of work, such as sociology or economics, may be sampled in a group of questions. Often these are principles which have become familiar to most persons through exposure rather than through formal training. It is difficult to advise you how to study for these questions; being alert to the world around you is our best suggestion.

2) Verbal ability

An example of an ability needed in many positions is verbal or language ability. Verbal ability is, in brief, the ability to use and understand words. Vocabulary and grammar tests are typical measures of this ability. Reading comprehension or paragraph interpretation questions are common in many kinds of civil service tests. You are given a paragraph of written material and asked to find its central meaning.

3) Numerical ability

Number skills can be tested by the familiar arithmetic problem, by checking paired lists of numbers to see which are alike and which are different, or by interpreting charts and graphs. In the latter test, a graph may be printed in the test booklet which you are asked to use as the basis for answering questions.

4) Observation

A popular test for law-enforcement positions is the observation test. A picture is shown to you for several minutes, then taken away. Questions about the picture test your ability to observe both details and larger elements.

5) Following directions

In many positions in the public service, the employee must be able to carry out written instructions dependably and accurately. You may be given a chart with several columns, each column listing a variety of information. The questions require you to carry out directions involving the information given in the chart.

6) Skills and aptitudes

Performance tests effectively measure some manual skills and aptitudes. When the skill is one in which you are trained, such as typing or shorthand, you can practice. These tests are often very much like those given in business school or high school courses. For many of the other skills and aptitudes, however, no short-time preparation can be made. Skills and abilities natural to you or that you have developed throughout your lifetime are being tested.

Many of the general questions just described provide all the data needed to answer the questions and ask you to use your reasoning ability to find the answers. Your best preparation for these tests, as well as for tests of facts and ideas, is to be at your physical and mental best. You, no doubt, have your own methods of getting into an exam-taking mood and keeping "in shape." The next section lists some ideas on this subject.

IV. KINDS OF QUESTIONS

Only rarely is the "essay" question, which you answer in narrative form, used in civil service tests. Civil service tests are usually of the short-answer type. Full instructions for answering these questions will be given to you at the examination. But in case this is your first experience with short-answer questions and separate answer sheets, here is what you need to know:

1) **Multiple-choice Questions**

Most popular of the short-answer questions is the "multiple choice" or "best answer" question. It can be used, for example, to test for factual knowledge, ability to solve problems or judgment in meeting situations found at work.

A multiple-choice question is normally one of three types—
- It can begin with an incomplete statement followed by several possible endings. You are to find the one ending which *best* completes the statement, although some of the others may not be entirely wrong.
- It can also be a complete statement in the form of a question which is answered by choosing one of the statements listed.

- It can be in the form of a problem – again you select the best answer.

Here is an example of a multiple-choice question with a discussion which should give you some clues as to the method for choosing the right answer:

When an employee has a complaint about his assignment, the action which will *best* help him overcome his difficulty is to
- A. discuss his difficulty with his coworkers
- B. take the problem to the head of the organization
- C. take the problem to the person who gave him the assignment
- D. say nothing to anyone about his complaint

In answering this question, you should study each of the choices to find which is best. Consider choice "A" – Certainly an employee may discuss his complaint with fellow employees, but no change or improvement can result, and the complaint remains unresolved. Choice "B" is a poor choice since the head of the organization probably does not know what assignment you have been given, and taking your problem to him is known as "going over the head" of the supervisor. The supervisor, or person who made the assignment, is the person who can clarify it or correct any injustice. Choice "C" is, therefore, correct. To say nothing, as in choice "D," is unwise. Supervisors have and interest in knowing the problems employees are facing, and the employee is seeking a solution to his problem.

2) True/False Questions

The "true/false" or "right/wrong" form of question is sometimes used. Here a complete statement is given. Your job is to decide whether the statement is right or wrong.

SAMPLE: A roaming cell-phone call to a nearby city costs less than a non-roaming call to a distant city.

This statement is wrong, or false, since roaming calls are more expensive.

This is not a complete list of all possible question forms, although most of the others are variations of these common types. You will always get complete directions for answering questions. Be sure you understand *how* to mark your answers – ask questions until you do.

V. RECORDING YOUR ANSWERS

Computer terminals are used more and more today for many different kinds of exams.

For an examination with very few applicants, you may be told to record your answers in the test booklet itself. Separate answer sheets are much more common. If this separate answer sheet is to be scored by machine – and this is often the case – it is highly important that you mark your answers correctly in order to get credit.

An electronic scoring machine is often used in civil service offices because of the speed with which papers can be scored. Machine-scored answer sheets must be marked with a pencil, which will be given to you. This pencil has a high graphite content which responds to the electronic scoring machine. As a matter of fact, stray dots may register as answers, so do not let your pencil rest on the answer sheet while you are pondering the correct answer. Also, if your pencil lead breaks or is otherwise defective, ask for another.

Since the answer sheet will be dropped in a slot in the scoring machine, be careful not to bend the corners or get the paper crumpled.

The answer sheet normally has five vertical columns of numbers, with 30 numbers to a column. These numbers correspond to the question numbers in your test booklet. After each number, going across the page are four or five pairs of dotted lines. These short dotted lines have small letters or numbers above them. The first two pairs may also have a "T" or "F" above the letters. This indicates that the first two pairs only are to be used if the questions are of the true-false type. If the questions are multiple choice, disregard the "T" and "F" and pay attention only to the small letters or numbers.

Answer your questions in the manner of the sample that follows:

32. The largest city in the United States is
    A. Washington, D.C.
    B. New York City
    C. Chicago
    D. Detroit
    E. San Francisco

1) Choose the answer you think is best. (New York City is the largest, so "B" is correct.)
2) Find the row of dotted lines numbered the same as the question you are answering. (Find row number 32)
3) Find the pair of dotted lines corresponding to the answer. (Find the pair of lines under the mark "B.")
4) Make a solid black mark between the dotted lines.

VI. BEFORE THE TEST

Common sense will help you find procedures to follow to get ready for an examination. Too many of us, however, overlook these sensible measures. Indeed, nervousness and fatigue have been found to be the most serious reasons why applicants fail to do their best on civil service tests. Here is a list of reminders:

- Begin your preparation early – Don't wait until the last minute to go scurrying around for books and materials or to find out what the position is all about.
- Prepare continuously – An hour a night for a week is better than an all-night cram session. This has been definitely established. What is more, a night a week for a month will return better dividends than crowding your study into a shorter period of time.
- Locate the place of the exam – You have been sent a notice telling you when and where to report for the examination. If the location is in a different town or otherwise unfamiliar to you, it would be well to inquire the best route and learn something about the building.
- Relax the night before the test – Allow your mind to rest. Do not study at all that night. Plan some mild recreation or diversion; then go to bed early and get a good night's sleep.
- Get up early enough to make a leisurely trip to the place for the test – This way unforeseen events, traffic snarls, unfamiliar buildings, etc. will not upset you.
- Dress comfortably – A written test is not a fashion show. You will be known by number and not by name, so wear something comfortable.

- Leave excess paraphernalia at home – Shopping bags and odd bundles will get in your way. You need bring only the items mentioned in the official notice you received; usually everything you need is provided. Do not bring reference books to the exam. They will only confuse those last minutes and be taken away from you when in the test room.
- Arrive somewhat ahead of time – If because of transportation schedules you must get there very early, bring a newspaper or magazine to take your mind off yourself while waiting.
- Locate the examination room – When you have found the proper room, you will be directed to the seat or part of the room where you will sit. Sometimes you are given a sheet of instructions to read while you are waiting. Do not fill out any forms until you are told to do so; just read them and be prepared.
- Relax and prepare to listen to the instructions
- If you have any physical problem that may keep you from doing your best, be sure to tell the test administrator. If you are sick or in poor health, you really cannot do your best on the exam. You can come back and take the test some other time.

VII. AT THE TEST

The day of the test is here and you have the test booklet in your hand. The temptation to get going is very strong. Caution! There is more to success than knowing the right answers. You must know how to identify your papers and understand variations in the type of short-answer question used in this particular examination. Follow these suggestions for maximum results from your efforts:

1) Cooperate with the monitor

The test administrator has a duty to create a situation in which you can be as much at ease as possible. He will give instructions, tell you when to begin, check to see that you are marking your answer sheet correctly, and so on. He is not there to guard you, although he will see that your competitors do not take unfair advantage. He wants to help you do your best.

2) Listen to all instructions

Don't jump the gun! Wait until you understand all directions. In most civil service tests you get more time than you need to answer the questions. So don't be in a hurry. Read each word of instructions until you clearly understand the meaning. Study the examples, listen to all announcements and follow directions. Ask questions if you do not understand what to do.

3) Identify your papers

Civil service exams are usually identified by number only. You will be assigned a number; you must not put your name on your test papers. Be sure to copy your number correctly. Since more than one exam may be given, copy your exact examination title.

4) Plan your time

Unless you are told that a test is a "speed" or "rate of work" test, speed itself is usually not important. Time enough to answer all the questions will be provided, but this does not mean that you have all day. An overall time limit has been set. Divide the total time (in minutes) by the number of questions to determine the approximate time you have for each question.

5) Do not linger over difficult questions

If you come across a difficult question, mark it with a paper clip (useful to have along) and come back to it when you have been through the booklet. One caution if you do this – be sure to skip a number on your answer sheet as well. Check often to be sure that you have not lost your place and that you are marking in the row numbered the same as the question you are answering.

6) Read the questions

Be sure you know what the question asks! Many capable people are unsuccessful because they failed to *read* the questions correctly.

7) Answer all questions

Unless you have been instructed that a penalty will be deducted for incorrect answers, it is better to guess than to omit a question.

8) Speed tests

It is often better NOT to guess on speed tests. It has been found that on timed tests people are tempted to spend the last few seconds before time is called in marking answers at random – without even reading them – in the hope of picking up a few extra points. To discourage this practice, the instructions may warn you that your score will be "corrected" for guessing. That is, a penalty will be applied. The incorrect answers will be deducted from the correct ones, or some other penalty formula will be used.

9) Review your answers

If you finish before time is called, go back to the questions you guessed or omitted to give them further thought. Review other answers if you have time.

10) Return your test materials

If you are ready to leave before others have finished or time is called, take ALL your materials to the monitor and leave quietly. Never take any test material with you. The monitor can discover whose papers are not complete, and taking a test booklet may be grounds for disqualification.

VIII. EXAMINATION TECHNIQUES

1) Read the general instructions carefully. These are usually printed on the first page of the exam booklet. As a rule, these instructions refer to the timing of the examination; the fact that you should not start work until the signal and must stop work at a signal, etc. If there are any *special* instructions, such as a choice of questions to be answered, make sure that you note this instruction carefully.

2) When you are ready to start work on the examination, that is as soon as the signal has been given, read the instructions to each question booklet, underline any key words or phrases, such as *least, best, outline, describe* and the like. In this way you will tend to answer as requested rather than discover on reviewing your paper that you *listed without describing*, that you selected the *worst* choice rather than the *best* choice, etc.

3) If the examination is of the objective or multiple-choice type – that is, each question will also give a series of possible answers: A, B, C or D, and you are called upon to select the best answer and write the letter next to that answer on your answer paper – it is advisable to start answering each question in turn. There may be anywhere from 50 to 100 such questions in the three or four hours allotted and you can see how much time would be taken if you read through all the questions before beginning to answer any. Furthermore, if you come across a question or group of questions which you know would be difficult to answer, it would undoubtedly affect your handling of all the other questions.

4) If the examination is of the essay type and contains but a few questions, it is a moot point as to whether you should read all the questions before starting to answer any one. Of course, if you are given a choice – say five out of seven and the like – then it is essential to read all the questions so you can eliminate the two that are most difficult. If, however, you are asked to answer all the questions, there may be danger in trying to answer the easiest one first because you may find that you will spend too much time on it. The best technique is to answer the first question, then proceed to the second, etc.

5) Time your answers. Before the exam begins, write down the time it started, then add the time allowed for the examination and write down the time it must be completed, then divide the time available somewhat as follows:
   - If 3-1/2 hours are allowed, that would be 210 minutes. If you have 80 objective-type questions, that would be an average of 2-1/2 minutes per question. Allow yourself no more than 2 minutes per question, or a total of 160 minutes, which will permit about 50 minutes to review.
   - If for the time allotment of 210 minutes there are 7 essay questions to answer, that would average about 30 minutes a question. Give yourself only 25 minutes per question so that you have about 35 minutes to review.

6) The most important instruction is to *read each question* and make sure you know what is wanted. The second most important instruction is to *time yourself properly* so that you answer every question. The third most important instruction is to *answer every question*. Guess if you have to but include something for each question. Remember that you will receive no credit for a blank and will probably receive some credit if you write something in answer to an essay question. If you guess a letter – say "B" for a multiple-choice question – you may have guessed right. If you leave a blank as an answer to a multiple-choice question, the examiners may respect your feelings but it will not add a point to your score. Some exams may penalize you for wrong answers, so in such cases *only*, you may not want to guess unless you have some basis for your answer.

7) Suggestions
   a. Objective-type questions
      1. Examine the question booklet for proper sequence of pages and questions
      2. Read all instructions carefully
      3. Skip any question which seems too difficult; return to it after all other questions have been answered
      4. Apportion your time properly; do not spend too much time on any single question or group of questions

5. Note and underline key words – *all, most, fewest, least, best, worst, same, opposite,* etc.
6. Pay particular attention to negatives
7. Note unusual option, e.g., unduly long, short, complex, different or similar in content to the body of the question
8. Observe the use of "hedging" words – *probably, may, most likely,* etc.
9. Make sure that your answer is put next to the same number as the question
10. Do not second-guess unless you have good reason to believe the second answer is definitely more correct
11. Cross out original answer if you decide another answer is more accurate; do not erase until you are ready to hand your paper in
12. Answer all questions; guess unless instructed otherwise
13. Leave time for review

b. Essay questions
1. Read each question carefully
2. Determine exactly what is wanted. Underline key words or phrases.
3. Decide on outline or paragraph answer
4. Include many different points and elements unless asked to develop any one or two points or elements
5. Show impartiality by giving pros and cons unless directed to select one side only
6. Make and write down any assumptions you find necessary to answer the questions
7. Watch your English, grammar, punctuation and choice of words
8. Time your answers; don't crowd material

8) Answering the essay question

Most essay questions can be answered by framing the specific response around several key words or ideas. Here are a few such key words or ideas:

M's: manpower, materials, methods, money, management
P's: purpose, program, policy, plan, procedure, practice, problems, pitfalls, personnel, public relations

a. Six basic steps in handling problems:
1. Preliminary plan and background development
2. Collect information, data and facts
3. Analyze and interpret information, data and facts
4. Analyze and develop solutions as well as make recommendations
5. Prepare report and sell recommendations
6. Install recommendations and follow up effectiveness

b. Pitfalls to avoid
1. *Taking things for granted* – A statement of the situation does not necessarily imply that each of the elements is necessarily true; for example, a complaint may be invalid and biased so that all that can be taken for granted is that a complaint has been registered

2. *Considering only one side of a situation* – Wherever possible, indicate several alternatives and then point out the reasons you selected the best one
3. *Failing to indicate follow up* – Whenever your answer indicates action on your part, make certain that you will take proper follow-up action to see how successful your recommendations, procedures or actions turn out to be
4. *Taking too long in answering any single question* – Remember to time your answers properly

IX. AFTER THE TEST

Scoring procedures differ in detail among civil service jurisdictions although the general principles are the same. Whether the papers are hand-scored or graded by machine we have described, they are nearly always graded by number. That is, the person who marks the paper knows only the number – never the name – of the applicant. Not until all the papers have been graded will they be matched with names. If other tests, such as training and experience or oral interview ratings have been given, scores will be combined. Different parts of the examination usually have different weights. For example, the written test might count 60 percent of the final grade, and a rating of training and experience 40 percent. In many jurisdictions, veterans will have a certain number of points added to their grades.

After the final grade has been determined, the names are placed in grade order and an eligible list is established. There are various methods for resolving ties between those who get the same final grade – probably the most common is to place first the name of the person whose application was received first. Job offers are made from the eligible list in the order the names appear on it. You will be notified of your grade and your rank as soon as all these computations have been made. This will be done as rapidly as possible.

People who are found to meet the requirements in the announcement are called "eligibles." Their names are put on a list of eligible candidates. An eligible's chances of getting a job depend on how high he stands on this list and how fast agencies are filling jobs from the list.

When a job is to be filled from a list of eligibles, the agency asks for the names of people on the list of eligibles for that job. When the civil service commission receives this request, it sends to the agency the names of the three people highest on this list. Or, if the job to be filled has specialized requirements, the office sends the agency the names of the top three persons who meet these requirements from the general list.

The appointing officer makes a choice from among the three people whose names were sent to him. If the selected person accepts the appointment, the names of the others are put back on the list to be considered for future openings.

That is the rule in hiring from all kinds of eligible lists, whether they are for typist, carpenter, chemist, or something else. For every vacancy, the appointing officer has his choice of any one of the top three eligibles on the list. This explains why the person whose name is on top of the list sometimes does not get an appointment when some of the persons lower on the list do. If the appointing officer chooses the second or third eligible, the No. 1 eligible does not get a job at once, but stays on the list until he is appointed or the list is terminated.

X. HOW TO PASS THE INTERVIEW TEST

The examination for which you applied requires an oral interview test. You have already taken the written test and you are now being called for the interview test – the final part of the formal examination.

You may think that it is not possible to prepare for an interview test and that there are no procedures to follow during an interview. Our purpose is to point out some things you can do in advance that will help you and some good rules to follow and pitfalls to avoid while you are being interviewed.

What is an interview supposed to test?

The written examination is designed to test the technical knowledge and competence of the candidate; the oral is designed to evaluate intangible qualities, not readily measured otherwise, and to establish a list showing the relative fitness of each candidate – as measured against his competitors – for the position sought. Scoring is not on the basis of "right" and "wrong," but on a sliding scale of values ranging from "not passable" to "outstanding." As a matter of fact, it is possible to achieve a relatively low score without a single "incorrect" answer because of evident weakness in the qualities being measured.

Occasionally, an examination may consist entirely of an oral test – either an individual or a group oral. In such cases, information is sought concerning the technical knowledges and abilities of the candidate, since there has been no written examination for this purpose. More commonly, however, an oral test is used to supplement a written examination.

Who conducts interviews?

The composition of oral boards varies among different jurisdictions. In nearly all, a representative of the personnel department serves as chairman. One of the members of the board may be a representative of the department in which the candidate would work. In some cases, "outside experts" are used, and, frequently, a businessman or some other representative of the general public is asked to serve. Labor and management or other special groups may be represented. The aim is to secure the services of experts in the appropriate field.

However the board is composed, it is a good idea (and not at all improper or unethical) to ascertain in advance of the interview who the members are and what groups they represent. When you are introduced to them, you will have some idea of their backgrounds and interests, and at least you will not stutter and stammer over their names.

What should be done before the interview?

While knowledge about the board members is useful and takes some of the surprise element out of the interview, there is other preparation which is more substantive. It *is* possible to prepare for an oral interview – in several ways:

1) Keep a copy of your application and review it carefully before the interview

This may be the only document before the oral board, and the starting point of the interview. Know what education and experience you have listed there, and the sequence and dates of all of it. Sometimes the board will ask you to review the highlights of your experience for them; you should not have to hem and haw doing it.

2) Study the class specification and the examination announcement

Usually, the oral board has one or both of these to guide them. The qualities, characteristics or knowledges required by the position sought are stated in these documents. They offer valuable clues as to the nature of the oral interview. For example, if the job involves supervisory responsibilities, the announcement will usually indicate that knowledge of modern supervisory methods and the qualifications of the candidate as a supervisor will be tested. If so, you can expect such questions, frequently in the form of a hypothetical situation which you are expected to solve. NEVER go into an oral without knowledge of the duties and responsibilities of the job you seek.

3) Think through each qualification required

Try to visualize the kind of questions you would ask if you were a board member. How well could you answer them? Try especially to appraise your own knowledge and background in each area, *measured against the job sought*, and identify any areas in which you are weak. Be critical and realistic – do not flatter yourself.

4) Do some general reading in areas in which you feel you may be weak

For example, if the job involves supervision and your past experience has NOT, some general reading in supervisory methods and practices, particularly in the field of human relations, might be useful. Do NOT study agency procedures or detailed manuals. The oral board will be testing your understanding and capacity, not your memory.

5) Get a good night's sleep and watch your general health and mental attitude

You will want a clear head at the interview. Take care of a cold or any other minor ailment, and of course, no hangovers.

What should be done on the day of the interview?

Now comes the day of the interview itself. Give yourself plenty of time to get there. Plan to arrive somewhat ahead of the scheduled time, particularly if your appointment is in the fore part of the day. If a previous candidate fails to appear, the board might be ready for you a bit early. By early afternoon an oral board is almost invariably behind schedule if there are many candidates, and you may have to wait. Take along a book or magazine to read, or your application to review, but leave any extraneous material in the waiting room when you go in for your interview. In any event, relax and compose yourself.

The matter of dress is important. The board is forming impressions about you – from your experience, your manners, your attitude, and your appearance. Give your personal appearance careful attention. Dress your best, but not your flashiest. Choose conservative, appropriate clothing, and be sure it is immaculate. This is a business interview, and your appearance should indicate that you regard it as such. Besides, being well groomed and properly dressed will help boost your confidence.

Sooner or later, someone will call your name and escort you into the interview room. *This is it*. From here on you are on your own. It is too late for any more preparation. But remember, you asked for this opportunity to prove your fitness, and you are here because your request was granted.

What happens when you go in?

The usual sequence of events will be as follows: The clerk (who is often the board stenographer) will introduce you to the chairman of the oral board, who will introduce you to the other members of the board. Acknowledge the introductions before you sit down. Do not be surprised if you find a microphone facing you or a stenotypist sitting by. Oral interviews are usually recorded in the event of an appeal or other review.

Usually the chairman of the board will open the interview by reviewing the highlights of your education and work experience from your application – primarily for the benefit of the other members of the board, as well as to get the material into the record. Do not interrupt or comment unless there is an error or significant misinterpretation; if that is the case, do not hesitate. But do not quibble about insignificant matters. Also, he will usually ask you some question about your education, experience or your present job – partly to get you to start talking and to establish the interviewing "rapport." He may start the actual questioning, or turn it over to one of the other members. Frequently, each member undertakes the questioning on a particular area, one in which he is perhaps most competent, so you can expect each member to participate in the examination. Because time is limited, you may also expect some rather abrupt switches in the direction the questioning takes, so do not be upset by it. Normally, a board member will not pursue a single line of questioning unless he discovers a particular strength or weakness.

After each member has participated, the chairman will usually ask whether any member has any further questions, then will ask you if you have anything you wish to add. Unless you are expecting this question, it may floor you. Worse, it may start you off on an extended, extemporaneous speech. The board is not usually seeking more information. The question is principally to offer you a last opportunity to present further qualifications or to indicate that you have nothing to add. So, if you feel that a significant qualification or characteristic has been overlooked, it is proper to point it out in a sentence or so. Do not compliment the board on the thoroughness of their examination – they have been sketchy, and you know it. If you wish, merely say, "No thank you, I have nothing further to add." This is a point where you can "talk yourself out" of a good impression or fail to present an important bit of information. Remember, *you close the interview yourself*.

The chairman will then say, "That is all, Mr. _____, thank you." Do not be startled; the interview is over, and quicker than you think. Thank him, gather your belongings and take your leave. Save your sigh of relief for the other side of the door.

How to put your best foot forward

Throughout this entire process, you may feel that the board individually and collectively is trying to pierce your defenses, seek out your hidden weaknesses and embarrass and confuse you. Actually, this is not true. They are obliged to make an appraisal of your qualifications for the job you are seeking, and they want to see you in your best light. Remember, they must interview all candidates and a non-cooperative candidate may become a failure in spite of their best efforts to bring out his qualifications. Here are 15 suggestions that will help you:

1) Be natural – Keep your attitude confident, not cocky

If you are not confident that you can do the job, do not expect the board to be. Do not apologize for your weaknesses, try to bring out your strong points. The board is interested in a positive, not negative, presentation. Cockiness will antagonize any board member and make him wonder if you are covering up a weakness by a false show of strength.

2) Get comfortable, but don't lounge or sprawl

Sit erectly but not stiffly. A careless posture may lead the board to conclude that you are careless in other things, or at least that you are not impressed by the importance of the occasion. Either conclusion is natural, even if incorrect. Do not fuss with your clothing, a pencil or an ashtray. Your hands may occasionally be useful to emphasize a point; do not let them become a point of distraction.

3) Do not wisecrack or make small talk

This is a serious situation, and your attitude should show that you consider it as such. Further, the time of the board is limited – they do not want to waste it, and neither should you.

4) Do not exaggerate your experience or abilities
   In the first place, from information in the application or other interviews and sources, the board may know more about you than you think. Secondly, you probably will not get away with it. An experienced board is rather adept at spotting such a situation, so do not take the chance.

5) If you know a board member, do not make a point of it, yet do not hide it
   Certainly you are not fooling him, and probably not the other members of the board. Do not try to take advantage of your acquaintanceship – it will probably do you little good.

6) Do not dominate the interview
   Let the board do that. They will give you the clues – do not assume that you have to do all the talking. Realize that the board has a number of questions to ask you, and do not try to take up all the interview time by showing off your extensive knowledge of the answer to the first one.

7) Be attentive
   You only have 20 minutes or so, and you should keep your attention at its sharpest throughout. When a member is addressing a problem or question to you, give him your undivided attention. Address your reply principally to him, but do not exclude the other board members.

8) Do not interrupt
   A board member may be stating a problem for you to analyze. He will ask you a question when the time comes. Let him state the problem, and wait for the question.

9) Make sure you understand the question
   Do not try to answer until you are sure what the question is. If it is not clear, restate it in your own words or ask the board member to clarify it for you. However, do not haggle about minor elements.

10) Reply promptly but not hastily
   A common entry on oral board rating sheets is "candidate responded readily," or "candidate hesitated in replies." Respond as promptly and quickly as you can, but do not jump to a hasty, ill-considered answer.

11) Do not be peremptory in your answers
   A brief answer is proper – but do not fire your answer back. That is a losing game from your point of view. The board member can probably ask questions much faster than you can answer them.

12) Do not try to create the answer you think the board member wants
   He is interested in what kind of mind you have and how it works – not in playing games. Furthermore, he can usually spot this practice and will actually grade you down on it.

13) Do not switch sides in your reply merely to agree with a board member
   Frequently, a member will take a contrary position merely to draw you out and to see if you are willing and able to defend your point of view. Do not start a debate, yet do not surrender a good position. If a position is worth taking, it is worth defending.

14) Do not be afraid to admit an error in judgment if you are shown to be wrong

The board knows that you are forced to reply without any opportunity for careful consideration. Your answer may be demonstrably wrong. If so, admit it and get on with the interview.

15) Do not dwell at length on your present job

The opening question may relate to your present assignment. Answer the question but do not go into an extended discussion. You are being examined for a *new* job, not your present one. As a matter of fact, try to phrase ALL your answers in terms of the job for which you are being examined.

Basis of Rating

Probably you will forget most of these "do's" and "don'ts" when you walk into the oral interview room. Even remembering them all will not ensure you a passing grade. Perhaps you did not have the qualifications in the first place. But remembering them will help you to put your best foot forward, without treading on the toes of the board members.

Rumor and popular opinion to the contrary notwithstanding, an oral board wants you to make the best appearance possible. They know you are under pressure – but they also want to see how you respond to it as a guide to what your reaction would be under the pressures of the job you seek. They will be influenced by the degree of poise you display, the personal traits you show and the manner in which you respond.

ABOUT THIS BOOK

This book contains tests divided into Examination Sections. Go through each test, answering every question in the margin. We have also attached a sample answer sheet at the back of the book that can be removed and used. At the end of each test look at the answer key and check your answers. On the ones you got wrong, look at the right answer choice and learn. Do not fill in the answers first. Do not memorize the questions and answers, but understand the answer and principles involved. On your test, the questions will likely be different from the samples. Questions are changed and new ones added. If you understand these past questions you should have success with any changes that arise. Tests may consist of several types of questions. We have additional books on each subject should more study be advisable or necessary for you. Finally, the more you study, the better prepared you will be. This book is intended to be the last thing you study before you walk into the examination room. Prior study of relevant texts is also recommended. NLC publishes some of these in our Fundamental Series. Knowledge and good sense are important factors in passing your exam. Good luck also helps. So now study this Passbook, absorb the material contained within and take that knowledge into the examination. Then do your best to pass that exam.

EXAMINATION SECTION

EXAMINATION SECTION
TEST 1

DIRECTIONS: Each question or incomplete statement is followed by several suggested answers or completions. Select the one that BEST answers the question or completes the statement. *PRINT THE LETTER OF THE CORRECT ANSWER IN THE SPACE AT THE RIGHT.*

1. The _____ system circulates blood, delivers nutrients to cells, and removes waste products, and consists of the heart, blood vessels, and blood.
   A. circulatory   B. lymphatic   C. endocrine   D. nervous

   1.____

2. Which of the following is the branch of medical science that is concerned with the function, structure, and diseases of muscles?
   A. Mycology   B. Myology   C. Kinesiology   D. Osteology

   2.____

3. The infraorbital artery which supplies blood to the muscles of the eye, the teeth, and upper lip is a branch of the _____ carotid.
   A. external   B. anterior   C. internal   D. superficial

   3.____

4. The pronator turns the hand inward making the palm face in a downward direction; the _____ turns the hand outward making the palm face in an upward direction.
   A. flexor   B. extensor   C. abductor   D. supinator

   4.____

5. The _____ nerves are the nerves that carry impulses from the brain to the arrector pili muscles.
   A. arrector   B. pili   C. sensory   D. motor

   5.____

6. The branch of anatomy that deals with the structure and function of bones is
   A. orthotics   B. esthiology   C. kinesiology   D. osteology

   6.____

7. The _____ artery is another name for the maxillary artery which branches out to the lower region of the face, mouth, and nose.
   A. nasal   B. angular
   C. major transverse   D. facial

   7.____

8. What body part contains the auricularis superior muscle, the auricularis anterior muscle, and the auricularis posterior muscle?
   A. Nose   B. Mouth   C. Ear   D. Eyes

   8.____

9. Which of the following is the non-moving portion of muscle attached to bone or fixed muscle?
   A. Genesis   B. Origin   C. Joint   D. Tendon

   9.____

10. The _____ nerve affects the skin of the scalp, forehead, upper eyelids, and eyebrows.
    A. supra-orbital
    B. radial
    C. mental
    D. infra-trochlear

11. For what reason are packs formulated?
    A. Skin nourishment
    B. Deep cleanse
    C. Eliminate impurities
    D. Dry and tighten the skin

12. How does glycolic acid function to assist with acne treatment?
    A. Opens up impaction
    B. Suppresses melanin production
    C. Increases antioxidant production
    D. Moisturizes deep tissues

13. Which of the following calms the skin and eliminates redness?
    A. Exfoliating brush machine
    B. Galvanic treatment
    C. Gel masks
    D. Lipids

14. Which of the following statements is TRUE when making cleansing pads?
    A. Scrunch them so they are soft
    B. Make sure edges are straight
    C. Make sure the edges are frayed
    D. Not a good practice to make your own cleansing pads

15. Sponges, gloves, and 4x4 gauze pads are considered
    A. impediments   B. disposables   C. equipment   D. garments

16. Which of the following has the benefits of tightening the pores, hydration, and reducing excess oil?
    A. Effleurage   B. Toners   C. Facial masks   D. Astringents

17. Which of the following statements is TRUE regarding non-setting masks? Remain moist and
    A. close pores better
    B. hydrates the skin
    C. work as a peel
    D. dehydrates the skin

18. In what manner do male and female skin-care programs compare?
    A. Male skin requires exfoliation less often.
    B. Male skin rarely requires professional care.
    C. Female skin requires moisturizing more often.
    D. Males and females have the same skin care needs.

19. For what purpose is a peppermint tea mask beneficial?
    A. Reduce redness for irritated skin
    B. Dehydrated skin
    C. Reduce dark spots on the skin
    D. Make mature skin appear more youthful

20. What should the skin care professional do once a facial is complete? 20.____
    A. Put used and soiled disposables in bowls in the dispensary.
    B. Put non-disposable implements in the biohazard container.
    C. Do a quick survey of retail sales and commissions.
    D. Conduct post-consultation and prepare the room for the next client.

21. All of the following conditions develop in hair follicles EXCEPT 21.____
    A. milia   B. open comedones
    C. blackheads   D. furuncles

22. Moles, chloasma, and tanned skin are all examples of which of the following? 22.____
    A. Birthmarks   B. Dermatitis
    C. Hypopigmentation D. Hyperpigmentation

23. Which of the following is another name for papules? 23.____
    A. Blackheads   B. Whiteheads
    C. Clogged pores   D. blemishes

24. _____ causes red, scaly patches of inflammation and excessive skin production which rapidly takes on a silvery-white appearance. 24.____
    A. Eczema
    B. Psoriasis
    C. Miliaria rubra
    D. Decreased sudoriferous gland function

25. _____ are masses of sebum trapped in the hair follicle. 25.____
    A. Boils
    B. Herpes
    C. Acne
    D. Comedones

KEY (CORRECT ANSWERS)

1.	A	11.	A
2.	B	12.	A
3.	C	13.	C
4.	D	14.	C
5.	D	15.	B
6.	D	16.	C
7.	D	17.	B
8.	C	18.	D
9.	B	19.	A
10.	A	20.	D

21. A
22. D
23. D
24. B
25. D

TEST 2

DIRECTIONS: Each question or incomplete statement is followed by several suggested answers or completions. Select the one that BEST answers the question or completes the statement. *PRINT THE LETTER OF THE CORRECT ANSWER IN THE SPACE AT THE RIGHT.*

1. Steatoma is commonly referred to as which of the following? 1.____
   - A. Pimples
   - B. Naevus
   - C. Sebaceous cyst
   - D. Basal cell carcinoma

2. Which of the following statements is TRUE regarding secondary lesions? 2.____
   Always develop
   - A. into scars
   - B. in later stages of disease
   - C. as a result of heredity
   - D. from an infection

3. Which of the following could result from overcleansing the skin with alkaline products? 3.____
   - A. Asteastosis
   - B. Rosacea
   - C. Hypopigmentation
   - D. Hyperpigmentation

4. Contagious skin diseases can be attributed to _____ influences. 4.____
   - A. chemical
   - B. thermal
   - C. microbiological
   - D. toxicological

5. Creating the illusion of better proportion by applying a darker foundation to the sides of the face, the cheeks, and the center of the face is an appropriate method for individuals with _____ shaped faces. 5.____
   - A. oval
   - B. oblong
   - C. diamond
   - D. square

6. Which of the following statements is TRUE regarding shaping eyebrows for a client with close-set eyes? 6.____
   - A. Eyebrows should not be extended past the outer corner of the eye.
   - B. A short distance should be kept between the eyebrows.
   - C. A distance between the eyebrows should be widened.
   - D. A very low arch should be creat4ed with the eyebrows.

7. Colors which can be viewed with the naked eye are contained in the 7.____
   - A. level system
   - B. color wheel
   - C. visible light spectrum
   - D. gradient system

8. With which of the following can you determine the ideal eyebrow shape for your client? 8.____
   - A. A ruler
   - B. A stencil
   - C. 2 lines
   - D. 3 lines

9. Where is the PROPER location for blush application? 9.____
   - A. At the temples
   - B. Just above the cheekbones
   - C. Just below the cheekbones
   - D. In the middle of the cheekbones

10. How wide is the face at eye level?
    A. 4 eyes wide
    B. 5 eyes wide
    C. 7 inches wide
    D. 10 inches wide

11. Which of the following statements is TRUE regarding makeup colors with yellow overtones?
    A. They are cool.
    B. They are warm.
    C. They are translucent.
    D. They are old and need to be disposed of.

12. Applying _____ to the area you desire to appear less prominent can minimize wide or prominent facial features.
    A. rouge
    B. darker foundation
    C. lighter foundation
    D. lighter setting powder

13. Which of the following are the two types of eyelashes?
    A. Long and short
    B. Faux and natural
    C. Permanent and temporary
    D. Band and individual

14. _____ color is produced when mixing a primary color with a secondary color.
    A. Tertiary
    B. Base
    C. Darker
    D. Opposing

15. The stratum _____ is the layer of the epidermis which lies above the stratum lucidum.
    A. corneum
    B. granulosum
    C. spinosum
    D. basale

16. Where would you start and end the cleansing process? Start at the _____ and end at the _____.
    A. chin; eyebrows
    B. chin; temples
    C. neck; eyebrows
    D. neck; temples

17. If pH neutral is 7 and your product is a pH of 9, how many times more alkaline is your product?
    A. 2
    B. 10
    C. 50
    D. 100

18. Which of the following are the bones that form the cheekbones?
    A. Nasal
    B. Temporal
    C. Zygomatic
    D. Calvaria

19. The _____ muscle is the muscle that covers the chest.
    A. external intercostal
    B. serratus anterior
    C. pectoralis major
    D. external oblique aponeurosis

20. Cell division is scientifically known as
    A. mitosis
    B. meiosis
    C. kyphosis
    D. cytosis

21. Which of the following is the LARGEST bone of the mouth region?
    A. Maxilla
    B. Styloid process
    C. Mandible
    D. Sphenoid

22. Which of the following is the study of skin diseases and histology?   22.____
    A. Epidemiology   B. Dermatology
    C. Hematology   D. Immunology

23. Which of the following is the causes of the majority of allergic reactions?   23.____
    A. Sun   B. Perfumes/Fragrances
    C. Detergents   D. Air pollution

24. The _____ muscle covers the bridge of the nose.   24.____
    A. buccinators   B. platysma   C. procerus   D. masseter

25. The _____ muscle covers the upper back and the back of the neck.   25.____
    A. trapezius   B. digastric
    C. splenius cervicis   D. levator scapulae

KEY (CORRECT ANSWERS)

1.	C		11.	B
2.	B		12.	B
3.	A		13.	D
4.	C		14.	A
5.	C		15.	A
6.	C		16.	D
7.	C		17.	D
8.	D		18.	B
9.	C		19.	C
10.	B		20.	A

21. C
22. B
23. B
24. C
25. A

TEST 3

DIRECTIONS: Each question or incomplete statement is followed by several suggested answers or completions. Select the one that BEST answers the question or completes the statement. *PRINT THE LETTER OF THE CORRECT ANSWER IN THE SPACE AT THE RIGHT.*

1. _____ are vehicles that help to spread agents onto the skin. 1.____
   A. Emollients   B. Deodorants   C. Astringents   D. Tinctures

2. Trichology is the scientific study of 2.____
   A. skin   B. fingernails   C. hair   D. pigment

3. The stratum _____ is the layer of skin which contains keratin. 3.____
   A. corneum   B. granulosum   C. spinosum   D. basale

4. _____ glands are responsible for excreting perspiration. 4.____
   A. Sebaceous   B. Sudoriferous
   C. Ceruminous   D. Pineal

5. _____ glands are responsible for excreting sebum. 5.____
   A. Sebaceous   B. Sudoriferous
   C. Ceruminous   D. Pineal

6. _____ glands, found mostly in the axillary and genital areas, secrete a milky protein and fat rich substance that provides excellent nutrients for microorganisms found on the skin. 6.____
   A. Eccrine   B. Ceruminous   C. Sebaceous   D. Aprocine

7. _____ glands produce clear perspiration consisting primarily of water, sales, and urea and secrete perspiration when external temperature or body temperature is high. 7.____
   A. Eccrine   B. Ceruminous   C. Sebaceous   D. Aprocine

8. _____ is a mixture of oily substances and fragmented cells that act as a lubricant and keeps hair from becoming brittle. 8.____
   A. Acne   B. Sebum   C. Blackhead   D. Whitehead

9. A(n) _____ is an accumulation of dried sebum, bacteria, and melanin from epithelial cells in the oil duct. 9.____
   A. Acne   B. Furuncle   C. Blackhead   D. Whitehead

10. Which of the following is the DEEPEST layer of the skin? 10.____
    A. Stratum spinosum   B. Stratum basale
    C. Papillary layer of the dermis   D. Reticular layer of the dermis

11. Which skin layer connects the dermis and the epidermis? 11.____
    A. Stratum spinosum   B. Stratum basale
    C. Papillary layer of the dermis   D. Reticular layer of the dermis

2 (#3)

12. A cluster of boils is defined as a   12.____
    A. furuncle   B. carbuncle   C. milia   D. acne

13. Acne is defined as an active infection in the _____ glands.   13.____
    A. Eccrine   B. Ceruminous   C. Sebaceous   D. Aprocine

14. Which of the following is a chronic skin condition characterized by facial redness, small and dilated blood vessels on facial skin, and swelling?   14.____
    A. Psoriasis
    B. Eczema
    C. Rosacea
    D. Milia

15. Which of the following, also called a milk spot or an oil seed, is a keratin-filled cyst that can appear just under the epidermis or on the roof of the mouth?   15.____
    A. Psoriasis
    B. Eczema
    C. Rosacea
    D. Milia

16. Which of the following is the broad muscle that extends from the chest and shoulder to the chin?   16.____
    A. Mentalis   B. Platysma
    C. Orbicularis Oris   D. Sternocleidomastoid

17. Collagen makes up what percentage of the dermis?   17.____
    A. 10%   B. 30%   C. 50%   D. 70%

18. The skin of which ethnic group is MOST prone to sensitivities?   18.____
    A. Caucasian   B. African-American
    C. Asian   D. Native American

19. The skin of which ethnic group is MOST prone to pigmentation problems?   19.____
    A. Caucasian   B. African-American
    C. Asian   D. Native American

3 (#3)

20. _____ is the technical name for eyelash hair. 20.____
    A. Cilia   B. Milia   C. Follicle   D. Furuncle

21. The Fitzpatrick Scale measures the skin's ability to tolerate which of the following? 21.____
    A. Heat   B. Cold   C. Moisture   D. Sun

22. What pathogenic agents are responsible for pus production? 22.____
    A. Bacteria   B. Fungi   C. Viruses   D. Prions

23. What form of skin cancer is characterized by pearly nodules? 23.____
    A. Melanoma
    B. Basal Cell Carcinoma
    C. Squamous Cell Carcinoma
    D. Kaposi's Sarcoma

24. Which plant has stimulating properties and is used for skin treatments? 14.____
    A. Peppermint   B. Eucalyptus   C. Camomille   D. Aloe

25. _____ is a plant extract that has soothing and calming properties. 15.____
    A. Peppermint   B. Eucalyptus   C. Chamomille   D. Aloe

KEY (CORRECT ANSWERS)

1. A
2. C
3. A
4. B
5. A

6. D
7. A
8. B
9. C
10. D

11. C
12. B
13. C
14. C
15. D

16. B
17. D
18. C
19. B
20. A

21. D
22. A
23. B
24. B
25. C

TEST 4

DIRECTIONS: Each question or incomplete statement is followed by several suggested answers or completions. Select the one that BEST answers the question or completes the statement. *PRINT THE LETTER OF THE CORRECT ANSWER IN THE SPACE AT THE RIGHT.*

1. Which of the following is the initial stages of hair production? 1._____
   A. Anagen   B. Catagen   C. Telogen   D. Teratogen

2. Which of the following is the final stage of hair production? 2._____
   A. Anagen   B. Catagen   C. Telogen   D. Teratogen

3. Which of the following is the purpose of a clay mask? 3._____
   A. Skin nourishment   B. Deep cleanse
   C. Eliminate impurities   D. Tone and tighten the skin

4. _____, also known as liver spots or senile freckles, refers to darkened spots on the skin caused by aging and the sun. 4._____
   A. Melasma   B. Vitiligo   C. Chloasma   D. Solar Lentigo

5. For what purpose would honey be used as a skin treatment? 5._____
   A. Skin nourishment   B. Deep cleanse
   C. Eliminate impurities   D. Tone and tighten the skin

6. What type of cell is responsible for immune protection of the skin? 6._____
   A. Keratinocytes   B. Melanocytes
   C. Merckle cells   D. Langerhan cells

7. _____ are the MOST common of the skin cells that account for between 90% and 95% of the skin. 7._____
   A. Keratinocytes   B. Melanocytes
   C. Merckle cells   D. Langerhan cells

8. _____ is the pigment that gives the skin its color. The darker the skin, the greater amount of this pigment is produced. 8._____
   A. Carotene   B. Melanin   C. Albumin   D. Anthocyanin

9. _____ is defined as the use of plants for therapeutic purposes. 9._____
   A. Herbal therapy   B. Aromatherapy
   C. Phytotherapy   D. Physiotherapy

10. What is the proper direction in which to clean the face of a man? 10._____
    A. Upward   B. Downward   C. Side to side   D. Circular

11. Which of the following are short, rod-shaped bacteria? 11._____
    A. Bacilli   B. Cocci   C. Spirilla   D. Typhi

12. _____ are pus-forming bacteria that grow in clusters like a bunch of grapes.
    A. Diplococci   B. Streptococci
    C. Staphylococci   D. Lactobacillus

13. Which of the following is the BEST stage to wax hair or perform electrolysis?
    A. Anagen   B. Catagen   C. Telogen   D. Teratogen

14. _____ is the process of introducing water-soluble products into the skin with the use of electric current such as the positive and negative poles.
    A. Anaphoresis   B. Cataphoresis
    C. Iontophoresis   D. Plasmaphoresis

15. What type of light therapy is used to relieve pain?
    A. Infrared   B. Visible   C. Ultraviolet   D. Cosmic rays

16. Which of the following is the surgical reduction of the upper and lower eyelids by removing excess fat, skin, and muscle?
    A. Mentoplasty   B. Blepharoplasty
    C. Otoplasty   D. Rhinoplasty

17. Vitamin _____ aids in the functioning and repair of skin cells and antioxidants.
    A. A   B. D   C. E   D. K

18. Vitamin _____ protects the cell membrane from harmful effects of the sun's rays which is found in green leafy vegetables, egg yolk, butter, and avocados?
    A. A   B. D   C. E   D. K

19. An itchy, swollen lesion such as hives, insect bites, bee stings, and allergic reactions are commonly referred to as a
    A. pustule   B. papule   C. wheal   D. tubercle

20. Which of the following is a small elevation on the skin that contains no fluid but may develop pus such as a pimple or wart?
    A. Papule   B. Vesicle   C. Tumor   D. Wheal

21. A skin sore or abrasion that penetrates the dermis, such as chapped lips, is referred to as
    A. fissure   B. keloid   C. scale   D. ulcer

22. Which of the following is a small blister or sac containing clear fluid such as poison ivy, poison oak, herpes, or chickenpox?
    A. Tumor   B. Vesicles   C. Pustule   D. Tubercle

23. The thick coarse hair that grows on the face to form a beard is known as
    A. barba   B. capilli   C. lanugu   D. terminial

24. Which of the following is an exfoliate that is rolled or massaged off?
    A. Enzymes   B. Chemicals   C. Scrubs   D. Gommage

25. Which of the following is the MOST commonly used technique for unblocking clogged pores and drives acidic solutions deeper into the epidermis and produces a chemical change? 25.____
    A. Galvanic treatment
    B. Anaphoresis
    C. Cataphoresis
    D. Iontoporesis

KEY (CORRECT ANSWERS)

1.	A		11.	A
2.	C		12.	C
3.	C		13.	A
4.	D		14.	C
5.	D		15.	A
6.	D		16.	B
7.	A		17.	A
8.	B		18.	C
9.	C		19.	C
10.	B		20.	A

21.	A
22.	B
23.	A
24.	D
25.	A

EXAMINATION SECTION
TEST 1

DIRECTIONS: Each question or incomplete statement is followed by several suggested answers or completions. Select the one that BEST answers the question or completes the statement. *PRINT THE LETTER OF THE CORRECT ANSWER IN THE SPACE AT THE RIGHT.*

1. In order to insure proper sanitation, all linens and draping used by a massage therapist must be washed in water that is AT LEAST _____ °F.   1.____

    A. 75   B. 98   C. 140   D. 212

2. What medical root word is NOT associated with the blood vessels?   2.____

    A. Vas   B. Yen   C. Arterio   D. Cyt

3. A client experiences acute pain from the neck down to the thigh.   3.____
   What condition would the client MOST likely have?

    A. Shoulder nerve impingement
    B. Volkmann's contracture
    C. Slipped disc
    D. Torticollis

4. Which of the following conditions is LEAST likely to provide for the opportunistic invasion of pathogenic bacteria?   4.____
   Changes in skin

    A. moisture   B. temperature   C. covering   D. pH

5. Which of the following factors would be the LEAST likely significant contributor to muscle fatigue?   5.____

    A. Lymphatic disturbances   B. Circulatory disturbances
    C. Excessive activity   D. Malnutrition

6. What type of articular disorder is caused by the over-accumulation of uric acid in the blood?   6.____

    A. Rheumatoid arthritis   B. Osteoarthritis
    C. Bursitis   D. Gouty arthritis

7. A client has an infection in the spongy tissue of a long bone, with a small inflammatory area.   7.____
   What condition would the client MOST likely have?

    A. Brodie's abscess   B. Necrosis
    C. Osteochondroma   D. Gouty arthritis

8. Each of the following procedures should be performed when cleaning the massage area EXCEPT   8.____

    A. shake out linen to free it of dust
    B. clean, brush or dust with strokes moving away from the body
    C. clean from the cleanest area to the dirtiest
    D. store used linens in a sealed container

15

9. What medical prefix denotes an abnormal condition? 9.____

   A. Para-   B. Peri-   C. Ab-   D. Mega-

10. Which of the following conditions is a consequence of muscle injury or degeneration? 10.____

    A. Fibrosis   B. Tendinitis
    C. Myopathy   D. Sprain

11. What is the medical term for softening of the muscle tissue? 11.____

    A. Dystrophy   B. Myomalacia
    C. Atrophy   D. Myelasia

12. Which of the following is a disinfection method? 12.____

    A. Pressurized steam bath
    B. Protective apparel
    C. Alcohol treatment
    D. Sanitary disposal of body tissues

13. What is the medical term for inflammation of the cartilage? 13.____

    A. Myectasis   B. Cyanitis
    C. Osteoplasty   D. Chondritis

14. The abnormal tissue *pannus*, which erodes joint cartilage, is associated with the disorder 14.____

    A. rheumatoid arthritis   B. osteoarthritis
    C. bursitis   D. gouty arthritis

15. Which of the following muscle disorders is caused by a tight-fitting bandage or cast? 15.____

    A. Volkmann's contracture   B. Torticollis
    C. Myosclerosis   D. Myasthenia gravis

16. Which of the following conditions is NOT standard for treatment of an immune-suppressed patient? 16.____

    A. Wearing disposable gloves
    B. Wearing a surgical mask or similar mouth covering
    C. Direct supervision by qualified physician
    D. Avoidance of direct contact with skin

17. A stroke or severe brain injury may cause a person to lose the ability to understand and/or express either spoken or written language. 17.____
    What is this condition called?

    A. Neuralgia   B. Aphasia
    C. Laryngemia   D. Amneosis

18. What type of muscle moves a body part toward the midline of the body? 18.____

    A. Levator   B. Tensor   C. Flexor   D. Adductor

19. What neural disorder causes a progressive destruction of the myelin sheaths of neurons?

    A. Multiple sclerosis
    B. Epilepsy
    C. Encephalitis
    D. Sciatica

20. A client suffers from a painful inflammation of the backbone. What condition would the client MOST likely have?

    A. Achondroplasia
    B. Brodie's abscess
    C. Osteomalacia
    D. Pott's disease

21. In order to insure proper sanitation, all linens and draping used by a massage therapist should be washed in a solution of

    A. 10% bleach
    B. 12% hydrogen peroxide
    C. 12% ammonia
    D. 15% lye

22. What is the medical term for pain in a joint?

    A. Chondrosis
    B. Osteolysis
    C. Ankylosis
    D. Arthralgia

23. What medical root word is associated with the head?

    A. Aden   B. Psych   C. Cephal   D. Rhin

24. Which of the following muscle disorders is caused by an acetylcholine defect?

    A. Volkmann's contracture
    B. Torticollis
    C. Muscular dystrophy
    D. Myasthenia gravis

25. Each of the following procedures should be performed by a massage therapist during handwashing EXCEPT

    A. clean under fingernails with a blunt orangewood stick
    B. keep fingers pointed slightly upward while washing
    C. use dry paper towel to turn off faucet
    D. interlace fingers to wash between them

KEY (CORRECT ANSWERS)

1. C
2. D
3. C
4. C
5. A

6. D
7. A
8. A
9. A
10. A

11. B
12. C
13. D
14. C
15. A

16. B
17. B
18. D
19. A
20. D

21. A
22. D
23. C
24. D
25. B

TEST 2

DIRECTIONS: Each question or incomplete statement is followed by several suggested answers or completions. Select the one that BEST answers the question or completes the statement. *PRINT THE LETTER OF THE CORRECT ANSWER IN THE SPACE AT THE RIGHT.*

1. Normal bone growth depends PRIMARILY on supplies of all of the following EXCEPT   1.____
    - A. iron
    - B. phosphorus
    - C. vitamin D
    - D. calcium

2. What type of bone/joint disorder is USUALLY limited to the destruction of joints and surrounding tissues?   2.____
    - A. Rheumatoid arthritis
    - B. Osteoarthritis
    - C. Tendinitis
    - D. Osteoporosis

3. Which of the following is an aseptic procedure for preventing the spread of pathogens?   3.____
    - A. Quarantine of affected patients
    - B. Pressurized steam bath
    - C. Wearing protective apparel
    - D. Disposal of body fluids or tissues

4. A vitamin D deficiency in adults that leads to demineralization of the bone tissue is   4.____
    - A. Paget's disease
    - B. rickets
    - C. osteitis
    - D. osteomalacia

5. What type of muscle straightens a body part?   5.____
    - A. Abductor
    - B. Extensor
    - C. Tensor
    - D. Flexor

6. In terms of sanitation and hygiene, what is the BEST material for a massage practitioner's uniform?   6.____
    - A. Wool
    - B. Vinyl
    - C. Polysynthetic
    - D. Cotton

7. Increased muscle irritability, accompanied by a decreased power in relaxation in the muscle, is a sign of   7.____
    - A. myosclerosis
    - B. gangrene
    - C. myopathy
    - D. myotonia

8. The inflammation of a nerve is MOST often caused by a deficiency in   8.____
    - A. cortisone
    - B. thiamine
    - C. iodine
    - D. riboflavin

9. In order to insure proper sanitation, any room used by a massage therapist should be able to maintain a room temperature of APPROXIMATELY_____°F.   9.____
    - A. 65
    - B. 75
    - C. 80
    - D. 85

10. What type of articular disorder is USUALLY caused by trauma?   10.____
    - A. Rheumatoid arthritis
    - B. Osteoarthritis
    - C. Bursitis
    - D. Gouty arthritis

11. What neural condition is denoted by acute inflammation caused by a virus that attacks the sensory cell bodies of dorsal root ganglia?

   A. Shingles
   B. Spina bifida
   C. Sciatica
   D. Neuralgia

11.____

12. Which of the following is NOT a method for sterilization?

   A. Steam bath
   B. Extreme temperature
   C. Radiation
   D. Chlorine treatment

12.____

13. Which of the following bone disorders is caused by *staph* bacteria?

   A. Osteomalacia
   B. Pott's disease
   C. Rickets
   D. Osteomyelitis

13.____

14. Weakened eye muscles and difficulty swallowing are early symptoms of

   A. Volkmann's contracture
   B. myasthenia gravis
   C. muscular dystrophy
   D. myosclerosis

14.____

15. What cleaning agent should be used if any body fluids come into contact with surfaces in a massage therapist's room during a session?

   A. Bleach solution
   B. Benzene
   C. Ammonia
   D. Ethyl alcohol

15.____

16. What is the medical term for inflammation of the nasal membrane?

   A. Nephritis
   B. Rhinitis
   C. Cyanitis
   D. Sinusitis

16.____

17. What type of articular disorder is MOST likely to lead to the creation of bone spurs?

   A. Rheumatoid arthritis
   B. Osteoarthritis
   C. Synovitis
   D. Gouty arthritis

17.____

18. Which of the following is NOT a recommended sanitation precaution for massage therapists?

   A. Avoid nail polish
   B. Use moisturizing lotion to prevent drying and cracking
   C. Fingernails should not extend over fingertips
   D. Hangnails should be covered during treatment

18.____

19. What disorder is caused by damage to the motor areas of the brain during fetal life?

   A. Cerebral palsy
   B. Epilepsy
   C. Muscular dystrophy
   D. Multiple sclerosis

19.____

20. Each of the following is a histological change associated with muscular dystrophy EXCEPT

   A. variation in fiber size
   B. mucous clogging of tissues
   C. deposition of fat
   D. degeneration of fibers

20.____

21. Which bone disorder is caused by a decrease in hormone output, which results in the decrease in the amount and strength of bone tissue? 21.____

    A. Osteoporosis
    B. Osteomyelitis
    C. Osteoma
    D. Osteomalacia

22. Which of the following materials is NOT considered to be a disinfectant? 22.____

    A. Alcohol
    B. Acetic acid
    C. Chlorine
    D. Detergent

23. What type of muscle moves a body part away from the mid-line of the body? 23.____

    A. Abductor   B. Levator   C. Flexor   D. Extensor

24. What is the medical term for a severe or complete loss of movement in a joint? 24.____

    A. Chondrosis
    B. Volkmann's contracture
    C. Ankylosis
    D. Arthralgia

25. What is considered to be the MOST effective deterrent to the spread of disease in a massage therapist's place of practice? 25.____

    A. Surface disinfectant
    B. Linen and draping washing
    C. Proper ventilation
    D. Handwashing

KEY (CORRECT ANSWERS)

1. A
2. A
3. B
4. D
5. B

6. D
7. D
8. B
9. B
10. C

11. A
12. D
13. D
14. B
15. A

16. B
17. B
18. B
19. A
20. B

21. A
22. B
23. A
24. C
25. D

EXAMINATION SECTION
TEST 1

DIRECTIONS: Each question or incomplete statement is followed by several suggested answers or completions. Select the one that BEST answers the question or completes the statement. *PRINT THE LETTER OF THE CORRECT ANSWER IN THE SPACE AT THE RIGHT.*

1. One way of inducing active immunity is to inject
    A. horse serum
    B. hormones
    C. streptomycin
    D. a vaccine

    1.____

2. Pus usually contains bacteria plus
    A. fungi
    B. scar tissue
    C. red blood cells
    D. white blood cells

    2.____

3. Among the major barriers to infection in the body are
    A. red blood cells
    B. striated muscle cells
    C. intestinal enzymes
    D. lymph nodes

    3.____

4. Salk polio vaccine consists of
    A. living virus
    B. killed virus
    C. virus plus antibodies
    D. virus plus sulfa drugs

    4.____

5. Pasteurization of milk
    A. destroys Vitamin C
    B. kills spore-forming bacteria
    C. is equivalent to sterilization
    D. involves boiling followed by cooling

    5.____

6. Botulism, a serious form of food poisoning, is MOST often due to
    A. unsatisfactory home canning
    B. undercooking of meat
    C. exposure of food to flies
    D. exposure of food to air

    6.____

7. All of the following foods may, if carelessly prepared, give rise to tapeworm infection EXCEPT
    A. beef   B. fish   C. fowl   D. pork

    7.____

8. Carriers are an important factor in the spread of
    A. diphtheria   B. pellagra   C. smallpox   D. beri beri

    8.____

9. Amebic dysentery may be prevented by the effective use of
    A. antibiotics
    B. immunization
    C. sewage disposal plants
    D. water chlorination

    9.____

10. Of the following diseases, the one transmitted by insects is
    A. influenza   B. trichinosis   C. pneumonia   D. typhus

    10.____

11. The _____ is NOT part of the brain.
    A. medulla B. cerebrum C. meristem D. all of the above

12. A cell is made up of
    A. fiber B. protoplasm C. nuclei D. cytoplasm

13. A cell is
    A. made of tissues
    B. the smallest living unit in the body
    C. the largest living unit in the body
    D. found only in the extremities

14. Organs are composed of
    A. bi-unitary cells
    B. singular cells
    C. tissue
    D. groupings of tissue

15. Red blood cells are made in the
    A. red marrow of your bones
    B. pancreas
    C. bloodstream
    D. white marrow of your bones

16. All cells get their material for their growth and repair from
    A. foods
    B. the same food
    C. minerals
    D. H_2O

17. A material essential to protoplasm is
    A. protein
    B. carbohydrate
    C. fat
    D. sugar and starch

18. As cell structures differ, so
    A. do the connective tissues
    B. does cell composition
    C. does the energy level
    D. does the oxygen required

19. Carbohydrates, proteins, fats, minerals, vitamins, and water are all
    A. cells B. energy C. chemicals D. nutrients

20. Scurvy can be prevented by
    A. vitamin C
    B. ascorbic acid
    C. green vegetables
    D. all of the above

21. A thermometer placed in your mouth for two minutes should NORMALLY read
    A. 96.6 B. 98.6 C. 98.7 D. 96.8

22. White blood cells
    A. are not necessary for life
    B. are all white
    C. counteract bacteria
    D. aid in digestion

23. The process of breaking down complex foods into simpler substances is called
    A. ingestion B. acidation C. digestion D. absorption

24. The heart pumps blood into the aorta. This is a(n) 24.____
    A. vein   B. artery   C. capillary   D. artery capillary

25. An INCORRECT statement about the heart is that it 25.____
    A. is made of thick muscle   B. pumps blood
    C. never stops   D. all are correct

26. Bright red blood can MOST likely be found in 26.____
    A. veins   B. arteries
    C. vein capillaries   D. all of the above

27. The kidney 27.____
    A. stores fatty foods   B. creates bile
    C. removes waste from the blood   D. stores proteins

28. Bacteria 28.____
    A. can thrive without food
    B. live and feed on other organisms
    C. are never seen
    D. all of the above

29. Bacteria can be 29.____
    A. helpful   B. protected against
    C. overcome   D. all of the above

30. Penicillin is made from 30.____
    A. mold   B. blue cheese
    C. cows' milk   D. roots of a penicillin tree

31. The rod-shaped bacteria are called 31.____
    A. cocci   B. spirilla   C. bacilli   D. viruses

32. A germ killer that is made by a living organism is called a(n) 32.____
    A. inoculation   B. toxin   C. antibiotic   D. streptococci

33. Vaccination or inoculation causes the human body to 33.____
    A. building antibodies   B. build toxins
    C. get well   D. have natural immunity

34. The part of the cell that controls all the functions of the cell is the 34.____
    A. nucleus   B. endoplasm   C. cytoplasm   D. cell membrane

35. _____ is an element. 35.____
    A. Steel   B. Brass   C. Copper   D. Bronze

KEY (CORRECT ANSWERS)

1.	D	11.	C	21.	B	31.	C
2.	D	12.	B	22.	C	32.	C
3.	D	13.	B	23.	C	33.	A
4.	B	14.	D	24.	B	34.	A
5.	A	15.	A	25.	D	35.	C
6.	A	16.	A	26.	B		
7.	C	17.	A	27.	C		
8.	A	18.	B	28.	B		
9.	C	19.	D	29.	D		
10.	D	20.	D	30.	A		

TEST 2

DIRECTIONS: Each question or incomplete statement is followed by several suggested answers or completions. Select the one that BEST answers the question or completes the statement. *PRINT THE LETTER OF THE CORRECT ANSWER IN THE SPACE AT THE RIGHT.*

1. In the human body, ciliated cells are found in the
   A. blood vessels
   B. small intestine
   C. lining of the trachea
   D. lining of the kidney tubules

   1.____

2. In the human digestive system, enzymes are produced for the digestion of all of the following EXCEPT
   A. cane sugar
   B. corn starch
   C. cellulose
   D. vegetable oils

   2.____

3. In the developing human embryo, respiration takes place through the
   A. gills   B. nostrils   C. lungs   D. placenta

   3.____

4. In the human embryo, the nervous system develops from the
   A. inner cell layer
   B. middle cell layer
   C. outer cell layer
   D. mesoderm

   4.____

5. The part of the eye affected in astigmatism is the
   A. cornea
   B. lens
   C. retina
   D. vitreous humor

   5.____

6. Dandruff is CHIEFLY composed of
   A. secretions of sebaceous glands
   B. dead epidermal cells
   C. yeast-like microbial organisms
   D. connective tissue from the scalp

   6.____

7. The white matter of the brain is made of
   A. nerve cell bodies
   B. axons and dendrites
   C. epithelial cells
   D. fat cells

   7.____

8. The behavior of a newborn child is characterized CHIEFLY by
   A. conditioned responses
   B. habit
   C. reflexes
   D. trial and error learning

   8.____

9. The organ that CANNOT be removed from the human body without causing death is
   A. the stomach
   B. the liver
   C. one kidney
   D. one lung

   9.____

10. A sphincter is a
    A. muscle that controls an opening
    B. joint of the ball-and-socket type
    C. gland producing both enzymes and hormones
    D. mass of nerve cells outside the spinal cord

11. The function of the parathyroid glands is to
    A. control calcium balance
    B. assure proper ovarian functions
    C. promote the digestion of starch
    D. aid in iron metabolism

12. The amount of blood in the body of an average man is normally _____ quarts.
    A. three   B. five   C. eight   D. ten

13. Red blood cells in the adult human being are formed in the
    A. bone marrow   B. liver
    C. lymph glands   D. heart

14. An artery containing blood relatively POOR in oxygen is the
    A. aorta   B. inferior vena cava
    C. superior vena cava   D. pulmonary

15. In tracer experiments designed to determine the length of life of red blood cells in the human body, the material used is an isotope of
    A. deuterium   B. gold   C. iron   D. phosphorus

16. A factor that is NOT necessary for the clotting of blood is
    A. prothrombin   B. air   C. calcium   D. fibrinogen

17. The structure that prevents food from passing into the windpipe is the
    A. esophagus   B. epiglottis   C. trachea   D. uvula

18. The HARDEST substance in the body is
    A. bone   B. cartilage   C. dentine   D. tooth enamel

19. The wrappings of the brain and spinal cord are
    A. epithelial tissues   B. meninges
    C. smooth muscles   D. striated muscles

20. The semicircular canals are PRIMARILY concerned with
    A. circulation of lymph   B. balance
    C. excretion   D. reproduction

21. Air pressure on both sides of the ear drum is equalized by the
    A. cochlea   B. ear bones
    C. Eustachian tubes   D. pharynx

22. Memory is dependent upon the function of the 22.____
    A. cerebral cortex   B. cerebellum
    C. medulla   D. spinal cord

23. The amount of light entering the eye is regulated by the 23.____
    A. cornea   B. iris   C. retina   D. sclerotic coat

24. An inherited characteristic of man controlled by more than one pair of 24.____
    genes is
    A. hemophilia   B. red-green color blindness
    C. blood type   D. brown or blue eye color

25. The epidermis of the skin 25.____
    A. contains numerous capillaries
    B. contains the coiled portions of sweat glands
    C. includes some living cells
    D. is where the hair roots are located

KEY (CORRECT ANSWERS)

1.	C	11.	A
2.	C	12.	B
3.	D	13.	A
4.	C	14.	D
5.	A	15.	C
6.	B	16.	B
7.	B	17.	B
8.	C	18.	D
9.	B	19.	B
10.	A	20.	B

21. C
22. A
23. B
24. C
25. C

TEST 3

DIRECTIONS: Each question or incomplete statement is followed by several suggested answers or completions. Select the one that BEST answers the question or completes the statement. *PRINT THE LETTER OF THE CORRECT ANSWER IN THE SPACE AT THE RIGHT.*

1. The daily energy requirement in calories recommended by the National Academy of Sciences for the average high school girl is
   A. 1300 – 1500   B. 2400 – 2600   C. 3000 – 3200   D. 4800 - 5000

   1.____

2. The recommended dietary protein allowance for an individual is LEAST influenced by the factor of
   A. sex
   B. age
   C. type of activity
   D. weight

   2.____

3. Of the following diseases, the one which is NOT food-borne is
   A. diphtheria
   B. pneumonia
   C. tuberculosis
   D. scarlet fever

   3.____

4. Of the following, the disease which is caused by an agent in a different group from the agents causing the other three diseases is
   A. tobacco mosaic disease
   B. typhus
   C. measles
   D. polio

   4.____

5. Of the following, the one which is a HIGHLY contagious skin condition is
   A. eczema
   B. hives
   C. impetigo
   D. miliaria rubra

   5.____

6. Of the following, the antibiotic that has been found MOST effective in the treatment of tuberculosis is
   A. penicillin
   B. aureomycin
   C. streptomycin
   D. tetracycline

   6.____

7. Toxic effects in children have resulted from the ingestion of excessive amounts of which one of the following?
   A. Vitamin A
   B. Vitamin B_{12}
   C. Vitamin C
   D. Thiamine

   7.____

8. The basal metabolism test is ordinarily used to indicate
   A. hypertension
   B. activity of the thymus gland
   C. activity of the thyroid gland
   D. rate of blood circulation

   8.____

9. When Vitamin B_{12} is administered by mouth, it is of little or no value unless
   A. it is part of the Vitamin B complex
   B. normal gastric juice is present
   C. it has been extracted from liver
   D. it is taken in capsule form

   9.____

10. The *morale vitamin*, the lack of which may cause people to become depressed and irritable, is   10.____
    A. ascorbic acid   B. thiamine   C. riboflavin   D. folic acid

11. Of the following, the tissue that lines the hair follicle is called   11.____
    A. dermis   B. epidermis   C. adipose   D. subcutaneous

12. Microscopic examination of the cross-section of hair shafts of people with straight hair shows the hair shafts to be   12.____
    A. square   B. flat   C. round   D. oval

13. The outer layer of the hair shaft is called the   13.____
    A. cortex   B. medulla   C. cuticle   D. papilla

14. Grain alcohol is converted into acetic acid by which one of the following processes?   14.____
    A. Oxidation   B. Reduction   C. Methylation   D. Esterification

15. Dark spots occurring in canned foods are often caused by   15.____
    A. reaction of tannin in the food and iron in the can
    B. overcooking the food
    C. oxidation of the tin coating of the can
    D. use of hard water in canning

16. Undercooked poultry may cause   16.____
    A. tularemia   B. brucellosis
    C. salmonella poisoning   D. trichinosis

17. Certain diseases must be reported to the Department of Health   17.____
    Which one of the following is NOT required to be reported?
    A. Pneumonia
    B. Food poisoning occurring in a group of three or more cases
    C. Meningitis
    D. Trichinosis

18. Food charts indicate the amount of Vitamin A in foods in terms of   18.____
    A. grams   B. International Units
    C. milligrams   D. micrograms

19. A hormone which is secreted by the adrenal glands and which equips animals to prepare for emergencies is   19.____
    A. insulin   B. epinephrine
    C. thyroxin   D. progesterone

20. In humans, maintenance of constant body temperature is a prime function of the   20.____
    A. endocrines   B. skin
    C. muscles   D. excretory system

21. At which one of the following sites does fertilization in humans USUALLY occur? 21.____
    A. Fallopian tube
    B. Graafian follicle
    C. Ovary
    D. Uterus

22. The pulse beat felt at the wrist is the immediate result of 22.____
    A. systolic pressure
    B. heart beat
    C. venous response to heart beat
    D. arterial pressure changes felt on the wall of the artery

23. Glycogen is stored in 23.____
    A. bone and cartilage
    B. fatty tissue
    C. liver and muscle
    D. small intestine

24. A drug discovered in clover hay that is used to prevent blood clotting is 24.____
    A. chloromycetin
    B. dicoumarin
    C. digitalis
    D. meprobamate

25. Which one of the following tissues has the GREATEST amount of intercellular matrix? 25.____
    A. Visceral muscle
    B. Connective tissue
    C. Nerve tissue
    D. Epithelium

KEY (CORRECT ANSWERS)

1.	B		11.	B
2.	C		12.	C
3.	C		13.	D
4.	D		14.	C
5.	C		15.	A
6.	C		16.	C
7.	A		17.	A
8.	C		18.	B
9.	B		19.	B
10.	A		20.	B

21. A
22. D
23. C
24. B
25. B

ANATOMY & PHYSIOLOGY
EXAMINATION SECTION
TEST 1

DIRECTIONS: Each question consists of a statement. You are to indicate whether the statement is TRUE (T) or FALSE (F). *PRINT THE LETTER OF THE CORRECT ANSWER IN THE SPACE AT THE RIGHT.*

1. A cell is a minute mass of protoplasm containing a nucleus. 1.____
2. Protoplasm is a jelly-like substance, present in all living matter. 2.____
3. Protoplasm is a lifeless matter. 3.____
4. Connective tissue serves to unite, support, and bind together other tissues. 4.____
5. Tendon is one of the varieties of connective tissue. 5.____
6. Muscle tissue is composed of cells modified to form fibers. 6.____
7. Organs are groups of systems. 7.____
8. Anabolism is the chemical change which involves the breaking down process within the cells. 8.____
9. Catabolism is the chemical change which involves the building up process within the cells. 9.____
10. Metabolism is the chemical change which involves the building up and breaking down process within the cells. 10.____
11. Nerves can be both motor and sensory. 11.____
12. Nerves can be stimulated by chemicals, massage, electricity, and heat. 12.____
13. Heat causes contraction of nerves. 13.____
14. Nervous fatigue is more prostrating than physical fatigue. 14.____
15. The cerebrum is the chief portion of the brain. 15.____
16. Nerves which carry information as to heat, cold, pressure, touch, and pain are called sensory nerves. 16.____
17. Sensory nerves and efferent nerves are the same. 17.____
18. The nervous system consists of cerebrospinal nervous system and the sympathetic nervous system. 18.____
19. The medulla oblongata is the bony structure protecting the brain. 19.____
20. Ganglia is a disease of the nervous system. 20.____

21. Nerves are a system of communication to all parts of the body.   21.___
22. Nerves have their origin in the brain.   22.___
23. Motor nerves carry impulses to the brain.   23.___
24. There are thirty-one pairs of cranial nerves.   24.___
25. There are fifteen pairs of spinal nerves.   25.___
26. The trifacial nerve is the smallest of all the cranial nerves.   26.___
27. The facial nerve is both motor and sensory.   27.___
28. The optic nerve is the nerve of the special sense of smell.   28.___
29. The mental nerve supplies lower lip and chin.   29.___
30. The temporal nerve supplies the frontalis muscle.   30.___
31. Mandibular nerve supplies the muscles of mastication.   31.___
32. The seventh pair of cranial nerves and the trifacial are the same.   32.___
33. The facial nerve supplies the muscles of expression in the face.   33.___
34. The lesser occipital nerve is a motor nerve.   34.___
35. The temporal is both sensory and motor nerve.   35.___
36. The blood vascular system controls the circulation of blood.   36.___
37. The walls of the arteries are elastic.   37.___
38. The veins lie deeper than the arteries.   38.___
39. General circulation is also known as systemic circulation.   39.___
40. Capillaries have thinner walls than arteries and veins.   40.___
41. About one-twentieth of the body weight is blood.   41.___
42. The heart is called an involuntary muscle.   42.___
43. Hemoglobin is the coloring matter of the red corpuscles.   43.___
44. Systemic circulation carries the blood from the heart to the lungs.   44.___
45. The blood carries oxygen to the cells and carbon dioxide from them.   45.___
46. Arteries carry the impure blood.   46.___
47. Study of the vascular system includes blood and lymph.   47.___
48. Red corpuscles attack germs that enter the blood.   48.___

49. Arteries, veins, and capillaries are tubular vessels. 49.____
50. A leucocyte is a red corpuscle. 50.____
51. Leucocyte is the technical term for white blood corpuscle. 51.____
52. Cardiac is the technical term for heart. 52.____
53. Circulation may be stimulated by physical and chemical means. 53.____
54. Lymph reaches parts of the body not reached by the blood. 54.____
55. The occipital artery supplies the forehead. 55.____

KEY (CORRECT ANSWERS)

1. T	11. T	21. T	31. T	41. T	51. T
2. T	12. T	22. T	32. F	42. T	52. T
3. F	13. F	23. F	33. T	43. T	53. T
4. T	14. T	24. F	34. F	44. F	54. T
5. T	15. T	25. F	35. T	45. T	55. F
6. T	16. T	26. F	36. T	46. F	
7. F	17. F	27. T	37. T	47. T	
8. F	18. T	28. F	38. F	48. F	
9. F	19. F	29. T	39. T	49. T	
10. T	20. F	30. F	40. T	50. F	

TEST 2

DIRECTIONS: Each question consists of a statement. You are to indicate whether the statement is TRUE (T) or FALSE (F). *PRINT THE LETTER OF THE CORRECT ANSWER IN THE SPACE AT THE RIGHT.*

1. The technical term for bone is os. 1.____
2. Bone is composed of animal and mineral matter. 2.____
3. Bone is pink externally and white internally. 3.____
4. The external membrane covering bone is called pericardium. 4.____
5. The shafts of long bones are solid. 5.____
6. The two types of bone tissue are dense and cancellous. 6.____
7. Dense tissue forms the interior of bone and cancellous tissue the exterior of bone. 7.____
8. The cranium is the bony case which encases the brain. 8.____
9. The skull is the technical term given the skeleton of the head. 9.____
10. The skull includes the cranial and the facial bones. 10.____
11. Red and white corpuscles are derived from red and yellow bone marrow. 11.____
12. Articulations and joints are the same. 12.____
13. Periosteum is a disease of the bone. 13.____
14. The entire skeleton consists of 106 bones. 14.____
15. The ends of bones are covered with cartilage. 15.____
16. The occipital bone is located at the crown. 16.____
17. The parietal bones are located at the forehead. 17.____
18. Maxillae are bones which form the upper jaw. 18.____
19. The cranium consists of ten bones. 19.____
20. The ethmoid is a small bone of the ear. 20.____
21. The malar bones form the prominence of the cheeks. 21.____
22. The turbinal bones form the eyesockets. 22.____
23. The mandible is the bone of the lower jaw. 23.____
24. The frontal bone forms the cheeks. 24.____
25. The temporal bones are located in the ear region. 25.____

26. Cartilage is sometimes called gristle. 26.____
27. Muscles are the active organs of locomotion. 27.____
28. The heart muscles are described as non-striated. 28.____
29. Voluntary muscles are controlled by the will. 29.____
30. The cardiac is a voluntary muscle. 30.____
31. Aponeurosis is a fibrous membrane. 31.____
32. Muscles may be stimulated by massage, heat, and electric current. 32.____
33. Striated muscles are involuntary. 33.____
34. Muscles are always connected directly to bones. 34.____
35. The muscular system relies upon the skeletal and nervous systems for its activities. 35.____
36. Contractility means able to be stretched or extended. 36.____
37. Muscles clothe and support the framework of the body. 37.____
38. The epicranius includes both the occipitalis and frontalis muscles. 38.____
39. The frontalis causes the forehead to wrinkle. 39.____
40. The occipitalis draws the scalp backward. 40.____
41. The levator palpebrae is the muscle that dilates the nostrils. 41.____
42. The orbicularis oculi is the muscle that surrounds the mouth. 42.____
43. The orbicularis oris is the muscle that surrounds the eye. 43.____
44. The trapezius muscle is a muscle of the face. 44.____
45. The temporalis is a muscle of mastication. 45.____
46. The masseter is a muscle that raises the lower jaw against the upper jaw. 46.____
47. The risorius is a muscle that retracts the angle of the mouth. 47.____
48. The sterno-cleido-mastoid muscle depresses and rotates the head. 48.____
49. The platysma is the large muscle in the back of the neck. 49.____
50. The trapezius is the muscle that raises the lower jaw. 50.____
51. The corrugator causes vertical wrinkles at the root of the nose. 51.____
52. The arrector pili is one of the largest muscles of the face. 52.____
53. The epicranius controls the movements of the scalp and wrinkles the forehead. 53.____

54. Muscles of the mouth are supplied by the facial nerve. 54.____

55. The deltoid muscle is a muscle of the lower back. 55.____

KEY (CORRECT ANSWERS)

1. T	11. T	21. T	31. T	41. F	51. T
2. T	12. T	22. F	32. T	42. F	52. F
3. F	13. F	23. T	33. F	43. F	53. T
4. F	14. F	24. F	34. F	44. F	54. T
5. F	15. T	25. T	35. T	45. T	55. F
6. T	16. F	26. T	36. F	46. T	
7. F	17. F	27. T	37. T	47. T	
8. T	18. T	28. F	38. T	48. T	
9. T	19. F	29. T	39. T	49. F	
10. T	20. F	30. F	40. T	50. F	

TEST 3

DIRECTIONS: Fill in the blanks with the MOST appropriate word from the set of words at the beginning of each section. Each answer may be used only once.

Questions 1-10.

tissues	circulatory	skeletal	growth
tendons	reproduction	muscular	nervous
cells	respiratory	organs	glandular

1. Fibrous tissues which connect muscles with bones are called _____.
2. The cytoplasm of the cell is essential for _____ and the nucleus is essential for _____.
3. Tissues are combinations of similar _____.
4. Organs are groups of two or more _____.
5. Systems are groups of _____.
6. The physical foundation of the body is the _____ system.
7. Contraction and movement are characteristic of _____ tissue.
8. The _____ system coordinates bodily functions.
9. The _____ system carries food to tissues and waste products from them.
10. The _____ system purifies the blood by the removal of carbon dioxide gas and the intake of oxygen gas.

Questions 11-20.

ligaments	flat	gristle	cancellous
mineral	dense	strength	immovable
sphenoid	shape	lacrimal	periosteum
cartilage	muscle	marrow	endosteum

11. Bone is composed of two-thirds _____ matter.
12. Bones are covered by a thin membrane known as _____.
13. The functions of the bones are to give _____ and _____ to the body.
14. The ends of bones are covered with _____.
15. The skull has _____ shaped bones and _____ joints.
16. The bone which joins all the bones of the cranium is the _____.
17. The _____ bones are the smallest and most fragile bones of the face.
18. Another name for cartilage is _____.

19. _____ are strong flexible or fibrous tissue that help to hold the bones together at the joints.

20. There are two types of bone tissue, namely _____ and _____.

Questions 21-28.

tendons	fascia	trapezius	aponeurosis
500	will	gristle	voluntary
fixed	myology	movable	mandible

21. The origin of a muscle refers to the more _____ attachment; whereas the insertion of a muscle applies to the more _____ attachment.

22. There are about _____ muscles in the body.

23. Muscles are joined to bones by means of glistening cords called _____.

24. A flat expanded tendon which serves to connect one muscle with another is called an _____.

25. A _____ is a membrane covering and separating layers of muscles.

26. The muscle which draws the head backward and sideways is the _____.

27. Voluntary muscles are put into action by the _____.

28. _____ is the study of the muscles.

Questions 29-38.

brain	cerebrospinal	digestion	blood
occipital	involuntary	maxillary	glands
muscles	sympathetic	trochlear	nerve
olfactory	mandibular	voluntary	accessory

29. Every muscle has its own _____ and _____ supply.

30. Sensory nerves carry impulses from the sense organs to the _____.

31. Motor nerves carry impulses from the brain to the _____.

32. The cerebrospinal nervous system controls the movements of _____ muscles.

33. The sympathetic nervous system controls the movements of _____ muscles.

34. The _____ nerve controls the movement of the superior oblique muscle of the eye.

35. The posterior auricular nerve supplies the _____ muscle.

36. The three main branches of the trigeminal nerve are the _____, _____, and _____.

37. The _____ system is under the control of the conscious will.   37.____

38. The _____ system controls the functions of circulation, digestion, and secretion of   38.____
    _____.

Questions 39-50.

superior vena cava	filtration	chest	oxygen
pulmonary veins	arteries	lungs	atrium
pulmonary arteries	ventricle	aorta	inferior
capillaries	bacteria	auricle	liquid

39. The main artery of the body is the _____.   39.____

40. _____ connect the smaller arteries with the veins.   40.____

41. The pulmonary circulation is the blood traveling to and from the heart and _____.   41.____

42. The red blood corpuscles carry _____ to the cells.   42.____

43. White blood cells destroy and devour harmful _____.   43.____

44. Plasma is the _____ portion of the blood.   44.____

45. Lymph is derived from the plasma of the blood by _____.   45.____

46. The upper chamber of the heart is called _____ or _____ and the lower chamber is   46.____
    known as a _____.

47. Vessels which carry blood from the extremities to the heart are called _____.   47.____

48. Vessels which carry blood from the heart to the lungs are called _____.   48.____

49. Vessels which carry blood from the lungs to the heart are called _____.   49.____

50. Vessels which carry blood from the heart to all parts of the body are called _____.   50.____

KEY (CORRECT ANSWERS)

1. tendons
2. growth, reproduction
3. cells
4. tissues
5. organs

6. skeletal
7. muscular
8. nervous
9. circulatory
10. respiratory

11. mineral
12. periosteum
13. strength, shape
14. cartilage
15. flat, immovable

16. sphenoid
17. lacrimal
18. gristle
19. ligaments
20. dense, cancellous

21. fixed, movable
22. 500
23. tendons
24. aponeurosis
25. fascia

26. trapezius
27. will
28. myology
29. nerve, blood
30. brain

31. muscles
32. voluntary
33. involuntary
34. trochlear
35. occipital

36. ophthalmic, maxillary, mandibular
37. cerebrospinal
38. sympathetic, glands
39. aorta
40. capillaries

41. lungs
42. oxygen
43. bacteria
44. liquid
45. filtration

46. atrium, auricle, ventricle
47. inferior, superior
48. pulmonary arteries
49. pulmonary veins
50. arteries

TEST 4

DIRECTIONS: In each set of questions, match the descriptions in Column II with the appropriate item in Column I. *PRINT THE LETTER OF THE CORRECT ANSWER IN THE SPACE AT THE RIGHT.*

COLUMN I | COLUMN II

Questions 1-5. Joints.

1. Condyloid   A. Spine   1.____
2. Hinge   B. Neck   2.____
3. Gliding   C. Wrist   3.____
4. Ball and socket   D. Hips   4.____
5. Pivot   E. Elbows   5.____

Questions 6-11. Cranial Bones.

6. Frontal   A. Between the orbits   6.____
7. Sphenoid   B. Ear region   7.____
8. Occipital   C. Crown of head   8.____
9. Ethmoid   D. Forehead   9.____
10. Temporal   E. Base of skull   10.____
11. Parietal   F. Base or brain and back of orbit   11.____

Questions 12-16. Facial Bones.

12. Malar   A. Cheek   12.____
13. Mandible   B. Septum of nose   13.____
14. Nasal   C. Upper jaw   14.____
15. Maxillae   D. Bridge of nose   15.____
16. Vomer   E. Lower jaw   16.____

COLUMN I	COLUMN II

Questions 17-23. Terms.

17.	Anterior	A.	On the side	17. ___
18.	Superior	B.	Situated lower	18. ___
19.	Posterior	C.	Situated higher	19. ___
20.	Inferior	D.	In front of	20. ___
21.	Levator	E.	In back of	21. ___
22.	Lateral	F.	That which enlarges	22. ___
23.	Dilator	G.	That which lifts	23. ___

Questions 24-29. Location of Muscles.

24.	Orbicularis oris	A.	Eyeball	24. ___
25.	Epicranius	B.	Ear	25. ___
26.	Rectus superior	C.	Neck	26. ___
27.	Procerus	D.	Scalp	27. ___
28.	Superior auricular	E.	Mouth	28. ___
29.	Platysma	F.	Nose	29. ___

Questions 30-37. Function of Muscles.

30.	Orbicularis oculi	A.	Opens eye	30. ___
31.	Orbicularis oris	B.	Rotates head	31. ___
32.	Levator palpebrae	C.	Rotates eyeball	32. ___
33.	Rectus muscle	D.	Wrinkles forehead	33. ___
34.	Depressor septi	E.	Contracts cheeks	34. ___
35.	Buccinator	F.	Opens and closes mouth	35. ___
36.	Sterno-cleido-mastoideus	G.	Closes eye	36. ___
37.	Epicranius	H.	Contracts nostrils	37. ___

COLUMN I

Questions 38-44. Function of Nerves.

38. Olfactory
39. Trigeminal
40. Glossopharyngeal
41. Accessory
42. Optic
43. Oculomotor
44. Auditory

Questions 45-52. Distribution of Nerves.

45. Infraorbital
46. Mental
47. Supraorbital
48. Palpebral
49. Lingual
50. Nasociliary
51. Auriculo-temporal
52. Ciliary

Questions 53-59. Terms.

53. Atrium
54. Fibrinogen
55. Hemoglobin
56. Lymphatics
57. Ventricle
58. Veins
59. Pericardium

COLUMN II

A. Sensory nerve of sight
B. Sensory-motor nerve of face and muscles of mastication
C. Sensory nerve of hearing
D. Controls movement of eyes
E. Sensory nerve of smell
F. Sensory-motor nerve of taste
G. Controls movement of trapezius muscle

A. Upper eyelid and forehead
B. Cornea and iris
C. Lower lip and chin
D. Nose
E. Nose and upper lip
F. Lower eyelids
G. Side of scalp
H. Tongue

A. A membrane enclosing the heart
B. Vessels which convey lymph
C. Upper cavity of the heart
D. Blood vessels containing valves
E. Coloring matter of red blood corpuscles
F. A substance essential for coagulation of blood
G. Lower cavity of the heart

38. ____
39. ____
40. ____
41. ____
42. ____
43. ____
44. ____

45. ____
46. ____
47. ____
48. ____
49. ____
50. ____
51. ____
52. ____

53. ____
54. ____
55. ____
56. ____
57. ____
58. ____
59. ____

COLUMN I	COLUMN II	

Questions 60-65. Distribution of Blood Vessels.

60. Orbital	A.	Back of ears and scalp	60.___
61. Septal	B.	Deeper portion of face	61.___
62. Posterior auricular	C.	Neck and back part of scalp	62.___
63. Superior labial	D.	Nostrils	63.___
64. Occipital	E.	Eye cavity	64.___
65. Internal maxillary	F.	Upper lip	65.___

KEY (CORRECT ANSWERS)

1.	C	16.	B	31.	F	46.	C	61.	D
2.	E	17.	D	32.	A	47.	A	62.	A
3.	A	18.	C	33.	C	48.	F	63.	F
4.	D	19.	E	34.	H	49.	H	64.	C
5.	B	20.	B	35.	E	50.	D	65.	B
6.	D	21.	G	36.	B	51.	G		
7.	F	22.	A	37.	D	52.	B		
8.	E	23.	F	38.	E	53.	C		
9.	A	24.	E	39.	B	54.	F		
10.	B	25.	D	40.	F	55.	E		
11.	C	26.	A	41.	G	56.	B		
12.	A	27.	F	42.	A	57.	G		
13.	E	28.	B	43.	D	58.	D		
14.	D	29.	C	44.	C	59.	A		
15.	C	30.	G	45.	E	60.	E		

EXAMINATION SECTION
TEST 1

DIRECTIONS: Each question or incomplete statement is followed by several suggested answers or completions. Select the one that BEST answers the question or completes the statement. *PRINT THE LETTER OF THE CORRECT ANSWER IN THE SPACE AT THE RIGHT.*

1. The basic functional unit of life is called a   1._____

   A. nerve
   B. cell
   C. molecule
   D. tendon

2. The study of the organization of tissues is called   2._____

   A. cytology
   B. embryology
   C. histology
   D. anatomy

3. Which of the following organelles plays a critical role in energy production in a eukaryotic cell?   3._____

   A. mitochondria
   B. Golgi apparatus
   C. nucleus
   D. ribosome

4. Which of the following is NOT a structure outside the cell wall?   4._____

   A. capsule
   B. flagella
   C. fimbriae
   D. endoplasmic reticulum

5. The most conspicuous organelle in a eukaryotic cell is the   5._____

   A. mitochondria
   B. nucleus
   C. Golgi apparatus
   D. ribosome

6. The region of the human body which contains the heart, lung, esophagus, thymus and pleura is the

A. abdomen
B. thorax
C. pelvis
D. neck

6._____

7. The thyroid is part of the _____ system.

A. circulatory
B. respiratory
C. endocrine
D. lymphatic

7._____

8. Which of the following is an autoimmune disorder whereby the body's own immune system reacts with the thyroid tissues in an attempt to destroy it?

A. postpartum thyroiditis
B. Hashimoto's disease
C. hypothyroidism
D. hyperthyroidism

8._____

9. The system of the body that contributes to balance and sense of spatial orientation is the _____ system.

A. vestibular
B. nervous
C. musculoskeletal
D. integumenary

9._____

10. An electrically excitable cell that processes and transmits information by electrical and chemical signaling is called a

A. synapse
B. tendon
C. neuron
D. tissue

10._____

11. How many bones does the hand contain?

A. 14
B. 22
C. 27
D. 31

11._____

12. Contractile tissue of animals derived from the mesodermal layer of embryonic germ cell is

A. tendon
B. muscle
C. bone
D. joint

13. The body part that forms the supporting structure of a human being is the

A. tendon
B. muscle
C. dermis
D. skeleton

14. The longest bone in the human body is the

A. patella
B. ulna
C. humerus
D. femur

15. The part of the body made up by the cervical, thoracic, and lumbar vertebrae is the

A. head
B. spine
C. arm
D. leg

16. All of the following are facial bones EXCEPT

A. phalanges
B. frontal
C. parietal
D. mandible

17. The human body is composed of approximately _____ muscles.

A. 125
B. 350
C. 640
D. 710

18. The science of the mechanical, physical, bioelectrical and biochemical functions of humans in good health, their organs and the cells of which they are composed is

A. cytology
B. anatomy
C. physiology
D. embryology

18._____

19. The organ system used for breathing and composed of the pharynx, larynx, trachea, bronchi, lungs and diaphragm is the _____ system.

A. respiratory
B. digestive
C. lymphatic
D. vestibular

19._____

20. The smallest of the body's blood vessels are the

A. veins
B. arteries
C. capillaries
D. villi

20._____

21. Arteries that carry deoxygenated blood to the heart and towards the lungs, where carbon dioxide is exchanged for oxygen are

A. pulmonary arteries
B. systemic arteries
C. arterioles
D. capillaries

21._____

22. An enclosed cable-like bundle of peripheral axons is called a

A. nucleus
B. vein
C. bone
D. nerve

22._____

23. The scientific generic name for a blood cell is a

A. erythrocyte
B. leukocyte
C. hematocyte
D. thrombocyte

23._____

24. Platelets have a lifetime of about 24._____

A. 24 hours
B. 1 day
C. 10 days
D. 1 month

25. Endocrine glands secrete 25._____

A. sweat
B. hormones
C. oils
D. enzymes

KEY (CORRECT ANSWERS)

1. B	6. B	11. C	16. A	21. A
2. C	7. C	12. B	17. C	22. D
3. A	8. B	13. D	18. C	23. C
4. D	9. A	14. D	19. A	24. C
5. B	10. C	15. B	20. C	25. B

TEST 2

DIRECTIONS: Each question or incomplete statement is followed by several suggested answers or completions. Select the one that BEST answers the question or completes the statement. *PRINT THE LETTER OF THE CORRECT ANSWER IN THE SPACE AT THE RIGHT.*

1. A group of unicellular organisms having characteristics of both plant and animals are

   A. fungi
   B. bacteria
   C. parasites
   D. mites

1._____

2. A small infectious agent that can replicate only inside the cells of living organisms is a

   A. spore
   B. dermophyte
   C. virus
   D. parasite

2._____

3. Bacteria can be found

   A. in the ocean
   B. on land
   C. in soil
   D. everywhere on Earth

3._____

4. There are approximately _____ bacteria on earth.

   A. 500 thousand
   B. 500 million
   C. 500 billion
   D. 5 nonillion

4._____

5. All of the following are diseases caused by pathogenic bacteria EXCEPT

   A. cholera
   B. syphilis
   C. influenza
   D. leprosy

5._____

6. Bacteria are now regarded as

   A. prokaryotes
   B. eukaryotes
   C. plants
   D. animals

6._____

7. The first bacteria to be discovered were 7._____

   A. round
   B. rod-shaped
   C. square
   D. triangular

8. Bacteria lack a(n) 8._____

   A. nucleus
   B. Golgi apparatus
   C. Endoplasmic reticulum
   D. all of the above

9. Rigid protein structures that are used for motility are 9._____

   A. flagella
   B. fimbriae
   C. pili
   D. macrophages

10. What kind of energy do phototrophs use? 10._____

    A. sunlight
    B. organic compounds
    C. inorganic compound
    D. oxygen

11. The first phase of bacterial growth is called the _____ phase. 11._____

    A. log
    B. lag
    C. stationary
    D. repair

12. Blood-sucking insects that transmit disease from one organism to another are known as 12._____

    A. viruses
    B. bacteriae
    C. vectors
    D. parasites

13. Generally, viruses are _____ bacteria. 13._____

    A. smaller than
    B. larger than
    C. the same size as
    D. more abundant than

14. The process by which a strand of DNA is broken and then joined to the end of a different DNA molecule is called

   A. genetic drift
   B. antigenic shift
   C. genetic recombination
   D. viral evolution

14._____

15. The process in which the viral capsid is removed is called

   A. attachment
   B. penetration
   C. uncoating
   D. replication

15._____

16. A process that kills the cell by bursting its membrane and cell wall if present is called

   A. lysis
   B. budding
   C. penetration
   D. modification

16._____

17. Replication of RNA viruses usually takes place in the

   A. nucleus
   B. cytoplasm
   C. Golgi apparatus
   D. endoplasmic reticulum

17._____

18. The _____ virus can cause cancer.

   A. herpes
   B. Epstein-Barr
   C. papilloma
   D. human immunodeficiency

18._____

19. All of the following are common human diseases caused by viruses EXCEPT

   A. influenza
   B. chicken pox
   C. cold sores
   D. strep throat

19._____

20. A biological term that describes a state of having sufficient biological defenses to avoid infection, disease or other unwanted biological invasion is called

   A. bacteriology
   B. immunity
   C. inoculation
   D. safety

20._____

21. T cells belong to a group of white blood cells called

   A. thrombocytes
   B. lymphocytes
   C. leukocytes
   D. erythrocytes

21._____

22. A substance that contains an antigen and is used to artificially acquire active immunity is known as a

   A. platelet
   B. vaccine
   C. serum
   D. venom

22._____

23. Parasitism is a type of _____ relationship between organisms of different species where one organism, the parasite, benefits at the expense of the other, the host.

   A. moral
   B. monogamous
   C. symbiotic
   D. mellifluous

23._____

24. Parasites that live on the surface of the host are called

   A. ectoparasites
   B. endoparasites
   C. epiparasites
   D. brood parasites

24._____

25. The most important measure for preventing the spread of pathogens is effective

   A. vaccination
   B. protective equipment
   C. hand washing
   D. isolation

25._____

KEY (CORRECT ANSWERS)

1. B	6. A	11. B	16. A	21. B
2. C	7. B	12. C	17. B	22. B
3. D	8. D	13. A	18. C	23. C
4. D	9. A	14. C	19. D	24. A
5. C	10. A	15. C	20. B	25. C

EXAMINATION SECTION
TEST 1

DIRECTIONS: Each question or incomplete statement is followed by several suggested answers or completions. Select the one that BEST answers the question or completes the statement. *PRINT THE LETTER OF THE CORRECT ANSWER IN THE SPACE AT THE RIGHT.*

1. Cocci are round-shaped 1.____
   A. viruses   B. fungi   C. bacteria   D. prions

2. Which of the following represents bacteria that can grow in pairs and cause pneumonia? 2.____
   A. Monococci   B. Diplococci   C. Gonococci   D. Streptococci

3. Failing to properly disinfect which of the following may cause a patient to break out due to the presence of Mycobacterium fortuitum? 3.____
   A. Styling chairs
   B. Shampoo stations
   C. Sharp instruments
   D. Whirlpool foot spas

4. Bacteria consists of an outer wall containing a liquid known as which of the following? 4.____
   A. Nucleic acid   B. Amino acid   C. Cytoplasm   D. Protoplasm

5. Which of the following refers to the process in which bacteria grow, reproduce, and divide into two new cells? 5.____
   A. Osmosis
   B. Meiosis
   C. Binary fission
   D. Binary fusion

6. A bacterial infection is characterized by the presence of which of the following? 6.____
   A. Pus   B. Mucous   C. Blood   D. Swelling

7. What type of infection would be characterized by a lesion containing pus and is confined to a particular part of the body? 7.____
   A. Local   B. Systemic   C. Primary   D. Secondary

8. Disinfectants used in salons must carry a registration number from what federal agency? 8.____
   A. Occupational Safety and Health Association
   B. Environmental Protection Agency
   C. Food and Drug Administration
   D. Department of Health and Human Services

9. What form of hepatitis is the MOST difficult to kill on a surface? 9.____
   A. A   B. B   C. C   D. D

10. Which of the following is defined as a submicroscopic particle that infects and resides in cells of biological organisms and is capable of replication only through taking over the reproductive functions of the host cell?
    A. Virus   B. Fungi   C. Prions   D. Bacteria

    10.____

11. Sterilization is the only form of decontamination that kills
    A. viruses   B. spores   C. fungi   D. bacteria

    11.____

12. Which of the following is a type of pathogenic bacteria?
    A. Flagella   B. Prions   C. Saprophytes   D. Parasites

    12.____

13. A _____ is a type of bacteria that lives on dead matter.
    A. parasite   B. macrophage   C. saprophyte   D. lymphocyte

    13.____

14. Syphilis and Lyme disease are caused by what agent?
    A. Cocci   B. Bacilli   C. Prions   D. Spirilla

    14.____

15. Bacilli are bacteria in what shape?
    A. Round   B. Oval   C. Rod   D. Corkscrew

    15.____

16. Spirilla are bacteria in what shape?
    A. Round   B. Oval   C. Rod   D. Corkscrew

    16.____

17. Which of the following are defined as slender, hair-like extensions in which certain bacteria about?
    A. Axons   B. Flagella   C. Fomites   D. Dendrites

    17.____

18. Which of the following is a difference between viruses and bacteria? Bacteria
    A. can penetrate cells   B. can become part of cells
    C. are resistant to antibiotics D. can live on their own

    18.____

19. Molds, mildew, and yeasts are all examples of which of the following?
    A. Fungi   B. Spores   C. Prions   D. Bacteria

    19.____

20. Removing pathogens and other substances from tools or surfaces is referred to as
    A. disinfection   B. decontamination
    C. sterilization   D. chemisorption

    20.____

21. Which of the following should be associated with every product used in a cosmetology school or salon?
    A. MSSDS sheet   B. FDA registration number
    C. Warning labels   D. Identification labels

    21.____

22. Which of the following statements is TRUE regarding any item that is used on a client?
    The item must be
    A. cleaned and sterilized
    B. either disinfected or discarded
    C. decontaminated and sterilized
    D. sanitized and disinfected

23. The majority of quaternary ammonium compounds are able to disinfect instruments in _____ minutes.
    A. 5-10
    B. 10-15
    C. 20-30
    D. 30-45

24. Phenolic disinfectants in 5% solution are primarily used for which of the following?
    A. Blood spills
    B. Rubber and plastic instruments
    C. Metal instruments
    D. Porous surfaces

25. States requiring hospital disinfection do not allow the use of which of the following for disinfection of instruments?
    A. Quaternary ammonium compounds
    B. Alcohol
    C. Phenols
    D. Antimicrobials

KEY (CORRECT ANSWERS)

1.	C	11.	B
2.	B	12.	D
3.	D	13.	C
4.	D	14.	D
5.	C	15.	C
6.	A	16.	D
7.	A	17.	B
8.	B	18.	D
9.	B	19.	A
10.	A	20.	B

21. A
22. B
23. B
24. C
25. B

TEST 2

DIRECTIONS: Each question or incomplete statement is followed by several suggested answers or completions. Select the one that BEST answers the question or completes the statement. *PRINT THE LETTER OF THE CORRECT ANSWER IN THE SPACE AT THE RIGHT.*

1. Which of the following represents the chemical name for bleach? Sodium
   A. hydroxide B. oxalate C. hypochlorite D. carbonate

   1._____

2. Which of the following products is considered unsafe for use in a salon because it can cause numerous health issues?
   A. Bleach B. Alcohol C. Formalin D. Antiseptics

   2._____

3. How often should the solution used in a wet sanitizer be changed and replaced?
   A. Hourly B. Daily C. Weekly D. Monthly

   3._____

4. In which of the following circumstances would an ultraviolet (UV) sanitizer be useful?
   A. Sterilizing instruments
   B. Disinfecting instruments
   C. Storing contaminated instruments
   D. Storing disinfected instruments

   4._____

5. Linens, capes, and drapes should be used once and then laundered with which of the following agents?
   A. Bleach B. Ammonia C. Phenols D. Antiseptics

   5._____

6. Which of the following statements is TRUE regarding instruments, such as hair clippers, that cannot be immersed in solutions?
   The instrument
   A. cannot be disinfected
   B. should be disinfected
   C. should be wiped with a wet cloth after use
   D. should be rinsed immediately after use

   6._____

7. How often should foot spas be disinfected with an EPA-registered disinfectant with bactericidal, fungicidal, virucidal, and tuberculocidal properties?
   A. Daily
   B. Weekly
   C. Bi-weekly
   D. After each client

   7._____

8. Bi-weekly (every 2 weeks), foot spas should be filled with what substance that should be left to sit overnight?
   A. Warm, soapy water
   B. Solution containing 5% bleach
   C. Solution containing 5% quaternary ammonium compound
   D. An EPA-registered disinfectant

   8._____

9. Washing your hands after each client is an example of which of the following?
   A. Sanitation   B. Disinfection   C. Sterilization   D. Contamination

10. Which of the following statements is TRUE regarding antiseptics? Antiseptics
    A. do not kill bacteria
    B. can be safely applied to the skin
    C. are classified as disinfectants
    D. are stronger than disinfectants

11. _____ is defined as the spread of infection from one person to another or from an object to a person.
    A. Direct transmission
    B. Airborne transmission
    C. Droplet transmission
    D. Cross-contamination

12. Which of the following are MOST resistant to cleansing agents?
    A. Viruses   B. Bacteria   C. Fungi   D. Prions

13. In order to be effective, the strength of ethyl alcohol must be no less than
    A. 50%   B. 60%   C. 70%   D. 80%

14. In order to meet salon requirements for use against bacteria, fungi, and viruses, a disinfectant should have the proper
    A. label
    B. efficacy
    C. concentration
    D. registration

15. What type of bacteria rarely exhibits any active motility?
    A. Cocci   B. Bacilli   C. Spirilla   D. Spores

16. The FIRST step in the decontamination process is referred to as
    A. rinsing   B. sanitation   C. disinfection   D. sterilization

17. Adherence to the bloodborne pathogen standard is regulated by what federal agency?
    A. Food and Drug Administration
    B. Centers for Disease Control and Prevention
    C. Environmental Protection Agency
    D. Occupational Safety and Health Administration

18. Which of the following refers to detergents that break down stubborn films and remove the residue of pedicure products such as scrubs, salts, and masks?
    A. Chelating agents
    B. Antifungal agents
    C. Antiseptic agents
    D. Virucidal agents

19. Which of the following is a corrosive, poisonous, acidic compound that is used as a disinfectant?
    A. Bleach   B. Ammonia   C. Phenols   D. Antiseptics

20. In what manner should you treat a salon instrument that comes into contact with blood or bodily fluids?
    The instrument should be cleaned and
    A. completely immersed in an EPA-registered disinfectant
    B. rinsed in an EPA-registered tuberculocidal antiseptic
    C. placed in an EPA-registered antiseptic that kills HIV and HepB
    D. briefly dipped in an EPA-registered solution that kills HIV

    20._____

21. For which of the following would the use of an antiseptic be effective?
    A. Sterilizing equipment
    B. Disinfecting equipment
    C. Decontaminating instruments
    D. Eliminating germs on the skin

    21._____

22. With regards to handwashing, for what time period should you apply soap, lather, and scrub your hands and under the free edges of the nail with a nail brush?
    A. 10 seconds   B. 20 seconds   C. 45 seconds   D. 60 seconds

    22._____

23. Which of the following is a recently approved form of disinfectant that only needs to be changed every 14 days?
    A. Formalin
    B. Glutaraldehyde
    C. Accelerated hydrogen peroxide
    D. Ethanol

    23._____

24. What type of disinfectants could potentially damage salon tools and equipment?
    A. Virucidal   B. Fungicidal   C. Bactericidal   D. Tuberculocidal

    24._____

25. Fungal infections are much more common on what area of the body than on the hands?
    A. Face   B. Scalp   C. Feet   D. Back

    25._____

KEY (CORRECT ANSWERS)

1. C
2. C
3. B
4. D
5. A

6. B
7. D
8. B
9. A
10. C

11. D
12. D
13. C
14. B
15. A

16. B
17. D
18. A
19. C
20. A

21. D
22. D
23. C
24. D
25. C

TEST 3

DIRECTIONS: Each question or incomplete statement is followed by several suggested answers or completions. Select the one that BEST answers the question or completes the statement. *PRINT THE LETTER OF THE CORRECT ANSWER IN THE SPACE AT THE RIGHT.*

1. If a disinfectant product includes the word _____ on the label, it must be diluted prior to use.
   A. solution B. concentrate C. catalyst D. hydrolyze

   1._____

2. Which of the following are various poisonous substances that are produced by some microorganisms?
   A. Prions B. Toxins C. Pathogens D. Carcinogens

   2._____

3. Which of the following repercussions can occur to a salon for not having MSDS sheets available for review during regular business hours?
   The salon
   A. can be fined
   B. can be closed
   C. can lose its license
   D. manager can be arrested

   3._____

4. What type of bacteria, as illustrated in the image shown at the right, grow in clusters similar to a bunch of grapes?
   A. Gonococci
   B. Streptococci
   C. Staphylococci
   D. Diplococci

   4._____

5. Which of the following statements is TRUE regarding bacteria during the spore-forming stage?
   Bacteria _____ during the spore-forming stage.
   A. grow in size
   B. perform mitosis
   C. are vulnerable to disinfectants
   D. coat themselves with wax outer shells

   5._____

6. Which of the following statements is TRUE regarding phenolic disinfectants?
   Phenolic disinfectants have a
   A. mildly alkaline pH
   B. neutral pH
   C. very low pH
   D. very high pH

   6._____

7. Regarding handwashing, what is the recommended method for brushing your nails?   7._____
   A. Diagonally
   B. Horizontally and vertically
   C. Vertically and diagonally
   D. Horizontally and diagonally

8. Which of the following is defined as the absence of disease-producing microorganisms?   8._____
   A. Sepsis   B. Asepsis   C. Immunity   D. Sterilization

9. Which of the following is defined as complete absence of all microorganisms?   9._____
   A. Sepsis   B. Asepsis   C. Immunity   D. Sterilization

10. A(n) _____ is defined as a microorganism capable of causing disease in humans.   10._____
    A. antigen   B. mutagen   C. pathogen   D. carcinogen

11. _____ is defined as the heightened ability of an organism to produce infection in its host.   11._____
    A. Persistence   B. Purulence   C. Virulence   D. Resistance

12. Which of the following is an additional term that refers to a germ or bacteria?   12._____
    A. Parasite   B. Microbe   C. Fomite   D. Dendrite

13. Which of the following refers to bacterial cells that are harmless and can even be beneficial to humans?   13._____
    A. Resistant bacteria
    B. Purulent bacteria
    C. Pathogenic bacteria
    D. Non-pathogenic bacteria

14. Nail fungus is a type of   14._____
    A. systemic infection
    B. external parasite
    C. pathogenic bacteria
    D. non-pathogenic bacteria

15. Which of the following is defined as the ability to destroy infectious agents that enter the body?   15._____
    A. Immunity
    B. Decontamination
    C. Disinfection
    D. Sterilization

16. Infection control can be divided into which of the following three categories?   16._____
    A. Bacteriology, ecology, virology
    B. Contamination, disinfection, sterilization
    C. Sanitation, disinfection, sterilization
    D. Bacteriology, virology, epidemiology

17. During a disinfection procedure, what should be done immediately following removing all hair from a brush?
The brush should be
   A. thoroughly dried
   B. washed with soap and water
   C. stored in a dry, covered container
   D. immersed in a disinfecting solution

17._____

18. Which of the following services would normally require a sterilization procedure when completed?
   A. Perming   B. Sculpting   C. Electrolysis   D. Shampooing

18._____

19. When performing first aid for a bleeding wound, what should be the NEXT step once the bleeding has stopped?
   A. Apply pressure   B. Apply bandage
   C. Apply tourniquet   D. Elevate affected limb

19._____

20. Bacteria grow BEST under what type of conditions?
   A. Cool, dry   B. Cool, damp   C. Warm, dry   D. Warm, damp

20._____

21. What is the FIRST thing to do when applying first aid to a chemical burn?
   A. Rinse away all traces of chemicals
   B. Apply cream or ointment to the burn
   C. Cover burn with a clean, dry cloth
   D. Immediately refer client to medical personnel

21._____

22. What is the FIRST thing to do when dealing with a heat burn and the skin is not broken?
   A. Apply ointment or cream to the burn
   B. Immerse burn in cool water or gently apply cool compresses
   C. Break the blister if one has formed
   D. Cover the burn with a clean, dry cloth

22._____

23. What is the FIRST thing to do if a client gets a salon chemical in their eyes?
   A. Flush eyes with cold water for 15-30 minutes
   B. Flush eyes with lukewarm water for 15-30 minutes
   C. Flush eyes with hot water for 15-30 minutes
   D. Place cloth over both eyes and secure with a bandage

23._____

24. Which of the following should be worn whenever there is a possibility of coming in contact with blood or other potentially infectious materials?
   A. Gloves   B. Gowns   C. Face masks   D. Goggles

24._____

25. What percentage of all bacteria are non-pathogenic?
   A. 30%   B. 50%   C. 70%   D. 90%

25._____

KEY (CORRECT ANSWERS)

1. B
2. B
3. A
4. C
5. D

6. D
7. B
8. B
9. D
10. C

11. C
12. B
13. D
14. C
15. A

16. C
17. B
18. C
19. B
20. D

21. A
22. B
23. D
24. A
25. D

TEST 4

DIRECTIONS: Each question or incomplete statement is followed by several suggested answers or completions. Select the one that BEST answers the question or completes the statement. *PRINT THE LETTER OF THE CORRECT ANSWER IN THE SPACE AT THE RIGHT.*

1. What type of immunity occurs when the body produces white blood cells and antitoxins to fight disease?   1.____
   A. Passive   B. Acquired   C. Natural   D. Herd

2. What should be the FIRST thing you do if a client sustains a burn severe enough to break the skin?   2.____
   A. Apply ointment or cream to the burn
   B. Immerse burn in cool water or gently apply cool compresses
   C. Notify medical personnel (call 911)
   D. Cover the burn with a clean, dry cloth

3. What is the FIRST thing you should do if a client suffers a cut, scratch, or embedded object in the eye?   3.____
   A. Attempt to remove the embedded object
   B. Immediately contact an eye specialist or emergency room
   C. Flush eyes with hot water for 15-30 minutes
   D. Place cloth over both eyes and secure with a bandage

4. Which of the following is a symptom of a first degree burn?   4.____
   A. Redness   B. Blisters   C. Skin rash   D. Skin charring

5. What tissue layer(s) are involved with a first degree burn?   5.____
   A. Epidermis only
   B. Dermis and epidermis
   C. Dermis and subcutaneous tissue
   D. Epidermis, dermis, and subcutaneous tissue

6. What is the FIRST thing you should do if you feel a client may be choking?   6.____
   A. Wrap arms around client
   B. Perform upward thrusts to client's abdomen
   C. Notify medical personnel (call 911)
   D. Determine if the client can talk

7. Infection can invade the body through all of the following EXCEPT   7.____
   A. nose   B. mouth   C. healthy skin   D. broken skin

8. As bacteria absorb food, each cell grows in size and divides, resulting in how many new cells?   8.____
   A. 2   B. 4   C. 6   D. 8

9. Which of the following is NOT effective in eliminating all organisms, is technically a sanitizer, and can also be used as a holding space for disinfected implements?
   A. UV light sterilizer
   B. Autoclave
   C. Chemiclave
   D. Gas sterilizer

10. Which of the following is a pressurized, steam-heated vessel that sterilizes with high pressure, heat, or pressurized steam preventing microorganisms from surviving?
    A. UV light sterilizer
    B. Autoclave
    C. Chemiclave
    D. Gas sterilizer

11. Which of the following uses high pressure, high temperature water, alcohol, and formaldehyde vapors for sterilization?
    A. UV light sterilizer
    B. Autoclave
    C. Chemiclave
    D. Gas sterilizer

12. What percentage of hydrogen peroxide can be used as an antiseptic?
    A. 1-3%
    B. 3-5%
    C. 5-10%
    D. 10-15%

13. Which of the following uses high-frequency sound waves to create a cleansing action that cleans areas on implements or tools that are difficult to reach with a brush?
    A. Autoclave
    B. Chemiclave
    C. UV light sterilizer
    D. Ultrasonic cleaners

14. At what point would the process referred to as "double bagging" be performed?
    A. When antiseptic is used
    B. When sharp objects are involved
    C. When a blood spill occurs
    D. When instruments cannot be decontaminated

15. A non-disposable needle used to puncture the skin requires what level of infection control?
    A. Sanitation
    B. Disinfection
    C. Decontamination
    D. Sterilization

16. Which of the following is the component of household bleach that kills viruses?
    A. Sodium
    B. Chlorine
    C. Fluorine
    D. Calcium

17. The active stage of bacteria is also known as the _____ stage.
    A. dormant
    B. reproductive
    C. vegetative
    D. duplicative

18. For effective disinfection, which of the following represents the MINIMUM strength of a quaternary ammonium compound solution to sanitize instruments?
    A. 1:100
    B. 1:250
    C. 1:500
    D. 1:1000

3 (#4)

19. Which of the following represents the MOST likely manner of HIV transmission in the salon or barbershop?
    A. Air   B. Droplet   C. Blood   D. Skin-to-skin

    19._____

20. All of the following are contagious diseases that will prevent a cosmetologist or barber from servicing a client EXCEPT
    A. ringworm
    B. common cold
    C. tuberculosis
    D. HIV/AIDS

    20._____

21. Due to production of potential harmful formaldehyde gas, which of the following should no longer be used in salons or barbershops?
    A. Sterilants
    B. Fumigants
    C. Disinfectants
    D. Decontaminants

    21._____

22. Which of the following represents the body's first layer of defense against transmission of disease?
    A. Skin   B. Hair   C. Nails   D. Tears

    22._____

23. It is recommended that a cosmetologist washes his/her hands with which of the following prior to servicing the client?
    A. Bar soap   B. Liquid soap   C. Antiseptic   D. Disinfectant

    23._____

24. Which of the following can be spread easily in a salon or barbershop through the use of unsanitary styling implements or from dirty hands or fingernails?
    A. Viruses
    B. Fungi
    C. Parasites
    D. Pathogenic bacteria

    24._____

25. What is the FIRST thing you should do if a client faints during treatment?
    A. Lay client on their back and allow plenty of fresh air
    B. Reassure client and apply cold compresses to face
    C. Roll client onto their side and keep their windpipe clear
    D. Call emergency personnel

    25._____

KEY (CORRECT ANSWERS)

1.	C	11.	C
2.	C	12.	B
3.	B	13.	D
4.	A	14.	C
5.	A	15.	D
6.	D	16.	B
7.	C	17.	C
8.	A	18.	D
9.	A	19.	C
10.	B	20.	D

21.	B
22.	A
23.	B
24.	D
25.	A

EXAMINATION SECTION
TEST 1

DIRECTIONS: Each question or incomplete statement is followed by several suggested answers or completions. Select the one that BEST answers the question or completes the statement. *PRINT THE LETTER OF THE CORRECT ANSWER IN THE SPACE AT THE RIGHT.*

1. Which of the following is the outermost layer of skin, sometimes referred to as cuticle or scarf skin, and does not contain any blood vessels?
    A. Dermis
    B. Epidermis
    C. Subcutaneous tissue
    D. Sclerodermis

    1.____

2. What underlying layer of skin is also referred to as derma curium cutis or true skin?
    A. Dermis
    B. Epidermis
    C. Subcutaneous tissue
    D. Sclerodermis

    2.____

3. In what layer of the epidermis does skin cell growth occur through mitosis or cell division? Stratum
    A. basale   B. lucidum   C. corneum   D. spinosum

    3.____

4. What layer of the epidermis is sometimes considered to be part of the stratum germinativum and includes cells that have absorbed melanin to distribute pigmentation to other cells? Stratum
    A. basale   B. lucidum   C. corneum   D. spinosum

    4.____

5. What layer of the epidermis is evident only on the palms of the hands and the soles of the feet where there are no hair follicles? Stratum
    A. basale   B. lucidum   C. corneum   D. spinosum

    5.____

6. What layer of the epidermis, sometimes called the horny layer, is the toughest part of the epidermis and composed of keratin protein cells that are continually shed and continually replaced by new cells below? Stratum
    A. basale   B. lucidum   C. corneum   D. spinosum

    6.____

7. What layer of skin is a fatty layer that acts as a shock absorber to protect the bones and to help support the delicate structures such as blood vessels and nerve endings?
    A. Dermis
    B. Epidermis
    C. Subcutaneous tissue
    D. Sclerodermis

    7.____

8. The _____ keeps the skin smooth, prevents dirt and grime from entering the outer layer of the epidermis, and also prevents the skin from drying or chapping.
    A. Acid mantle
    B. Dermis
    C. Subcutaneous tissue
    D. Sebaceous glands

    8.____

9. Which of the following is distributed through all epidermal cells and forms an effective barrier from the penetration of ultraviolet rays to the deeper layers of the skin and tans the skin to protect it from burning rays of the sun?

    A. Albumin   B. Keratin   C. Melanin   D. Collagen

9._____

10. Which enzyme found in melanosomes is important for the production of melanin?

    A. Lipase   B. Kinase   C. Tyrosinase   D. Peroxidase

10._____

11. Which of the following, illustrated in the image shown at the right, is characterized by a pigmented or erythematous, flat lesion on the epidermis?
    A. Macule
    B. Papule
    C. Nodule
    D. Vesicle

11._____

12. Which of the following, illustrated in the image shown at the right, is characterized by a peaked or dome-shaped surface lesion measuring less than 5mm in diameter?
    A. Macule
    B. Papule
    C. Nodule
    D. Vesicle

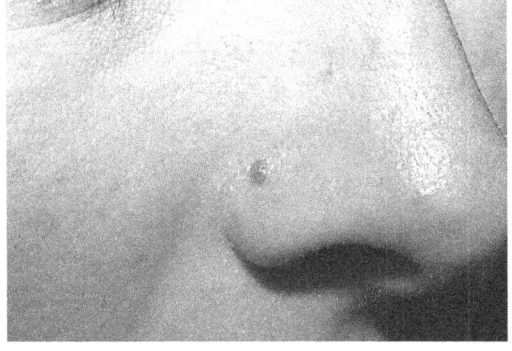

12._____

13. What skin disorder, illustrated in the image shown at the right, is characterized by an elevated, dome-shaped lesion greater than 5 mm in diameter?
    A. Nodule
    B. Plaque
    C. Vesicle
    D. Bulla

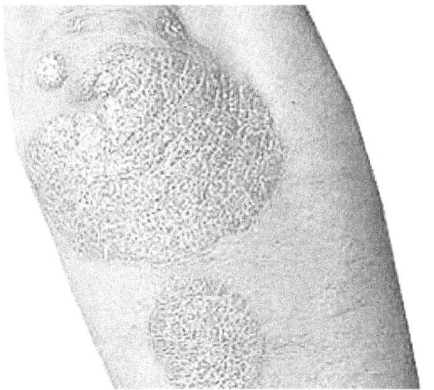

13._____

14. What skin disorder, illustrated in the image shown at the right, is characterized by fluid-filled blisters less than 5 mm in diameter?
    A. Nodule
    B. Plaque
    C. Vesicle
    D. Bulla

14.____

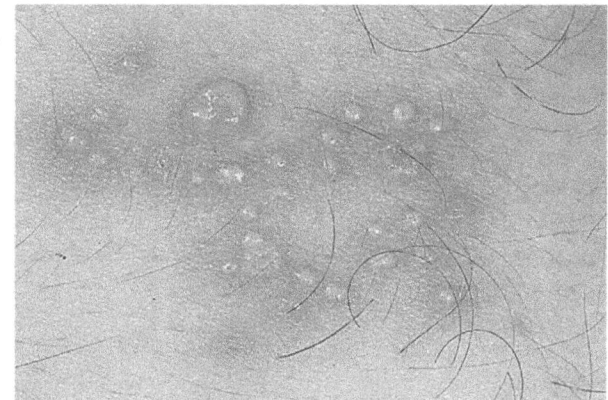

15. What skin disorder, illustrated in the image shown at the right, is characterized by fluid-filled blisters greater than 5 mm in diameter?
    A. Nodule
    B. Plaque
    C. Vesicle
    D. Bulla

15.____

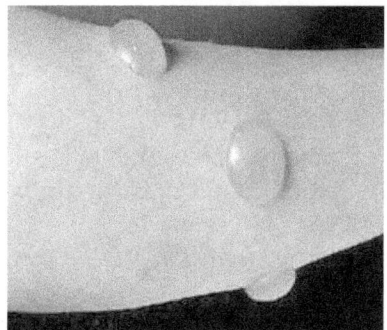

16. As illustrated in the image shown at the right, a wheal is an edematous, transient papule or plaque caused by fluid infiltration in what layer of the skin?
    A. Dermis
    B. Epidermis
    C. Sclerodermis
    D. Subcutaneous tissue

16.____

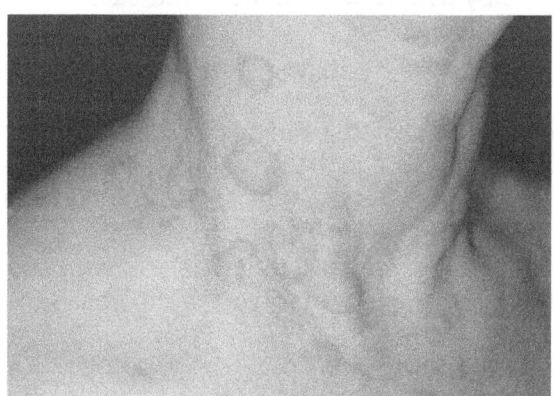

17. What skin disorder, illustrated in the image shown at the right, is characterized by fluid-filled blisters with inflammatory cells?
    A. Scales
    B. Pustules
    C. Vesicles
    D. Bulla

17.____

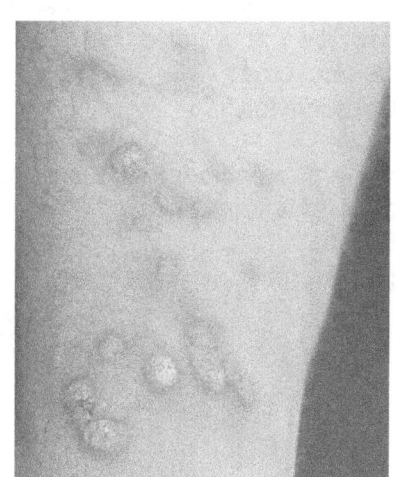

18. Hyperkeratosis, as illustrated in the image shown at the right, is characterized by increased thickness of what layer of the epidermis producing a scaled appearance on the skin?
    A. Stratum basale
    B. Stratum lucidum
    C. Stratum corneum
    D. Stratum spinosum

18._____

19. Which of the following is defined as intercellular connections made of proteins and are structures that assist in holding cells together?
    A. Desmosomes
    B. Melanosomes
    C. Corneocytes
    D. Keratinocytes

19._____

20. What type of melanin is red and yellow in color and normally produced by people with light-colored skin?
    A. Eumelanin
    B. Pheomelanin
    C. Neuromelanin
    D. Tyromelanin

20._____

21. What type of melanin is dark brown to black in color and is normally produced by people with dark-colored skin?
    A. Eumelanin
    B. Pheomelanin
    C. Neuromelanin
    D. Tyromelanin

21._____

22. Which of the following is defined as a fibrous, connective tissue made from protein that is found in the reticular layer of the dermis?
    A. Elastin   B. Collagen   C. Melanin   D. Keratin

22._____

23. Which of the following is defined as epidermal cells that are composed of keratin, lipids, and other proteins that comprise 95% of the epidermis?
    A. Desmosomes
    B. Melanosomes
    C. Corneocytes
    D. Keratinocytes

23._____

24. Which of the following is defined as hardened, waterproof, protective keratinocytes that are dried out "dead" protein cells that lack nuclei?
    A. Desmosomes
    B. Leukocytes
    C. Corneocytes
    D. Melanocytes

24._____

25. Elastin is a protein fiber found in what layer of the skin that gives skin its elasticity and firmness?
    A. Dermis
    B. Epidermis
    C. Hypodermis
    D. Subcutaneous tissue

25._____

KEY (CORRECT ANSWERS)

1.	B		11.	A
2.	A		12.	B
3.	A		13.	B
4.	D		14.	C
5.	B		15.	D
6.	C		16.	A
7.	C		17.	B
8.	A		18.	C
9.	C		19.	A
10.	C		20.	B

21. A
22. B
23. D
24. C
25. A

TEST 2

DIRECTIONS: Each question or incomplete statement is followed by several suggested answers or completions. Select the one that BEST answers the question or completes the statement. *PRINT THE LETTER OF THE CORRECT ANSWER IN THE SPACE AT THE RIGHT.*

1. Which of the following types of cells are located in the dermis and respond to allergies by releasing histamines?
   A. Mast   B. Merkel   C. Leukocytes   D. Langerhans

   1.____

2. Which skin condition, illustrated in the image shown at the right, is an acquired skin disease characterized by white patches caused by a loss of pigment?
   A. Vitiligo
   B. Lentigo
   C. Albinism
   D. Leukoderma

   2.____

3. A "blister" is another name for which of the following?
   A. Cyst   B. Pustule   C. Papule   D. Vesicle

   3.____

4. _____ is defined as the mechanical or chemical process of removing dead skin to stimulate new cell growth.
   A. Desquamation   B. Exfoliation
   C. Permeation   D. Hydrolysis

   4.____

5. What skin condition, as illustrated in the image shown at the right, is a pigmentation disorder commonly referred to as a freckle?
   A. Nevus
   B. Vitiligo
   C. Lentigo
   D. Scleroderma

   5.____

6. What region of the body can be characterized by the absence of apocrine glands?
   A. The nipples   B. The genitals
   C. The armpits   D. The soles of the feet

   6.____

7. Which of the following is a medical condition that results in the failure of the skin to produce melanin?
   A. Vitiligo   B. Albinism   C. Leukoderma   D. Scleroderma

7.____

8. _____ are the receptors responsible for reporting deep pressure and pain.
   A. Thermoreceptors
   B. Ruffini's corpuscles
   C. Pacinian corpuscles
   D. Meissner's corpuscles

8.____

9. _____ are the receptors responsible for reporting long-term pressure and heat.
   A. Chemoreceptors
   B. Ruffini's corpuscles
   C. Pacinian corpuscles
   D. Meissner's corpuscles

9.____

10. If a patient has a verruca on their skin, what is present on their skin?
    A. Wart   B. Pimple   C. Rash   D. Abrasion

10.____

11. _____ are the receptors responsible for reporting light pressure and cold.
    A. Krause's end bulbs
    B. Ruffini's corpuscles
    C. Pacinian corpuscles
    D. Meissner's corpuscles

11.____

12. Langerhans cells, which help protect the body from infection, are found in the stratum _____ layer of the skin.
    A. basale   B. lucidum   C. corneum   D. spinosum

12.____

13. Which of the following is defined as a male hormone that is found in both men and women that influences the amount of sebum that is produced?
    A. Melanin   B. Keratin   C. Collagen   D. Androgen

13.____

14. Which of the following is produced by the sudoriferous glands?
    A. Pus   B. Water   C. Sweat   D. Sebum

14.____

15. _____ is defined as the chemical conversion of living cells into dead protein.
    A. Desquamation
    B. Exfoliation
    C. Permeation
    D. Keratinization

15.____

16. Which pigment disorder, as illustrated in the image shown at the right, is commonly referred to as a birthmark?
    A. Nevus
    B. Vitiligo
    C. Lentigo
    D. Scleroderma

16.____

17. Which of the following is a medical condition caused by excess secretion of the sebaceous glands commonly associated with oily skin types?
    A. Hyperhidrosis   B. Seborrhea   C. Steatoma   D. Anhidrosis

17.____

18. _____ is defined as a mechanical abrasion of the epidermis that occurs when insect bites, scabs, or acne breakouts are scratched?
    A. Desquamation   B. Exfoliation
    C. Excoriation   D. Keratinization

18.____

19. Which of the following refers to an allergic reaction that produces an eruption of wheals?
    A. Hives   B. Carbuncle   C. Acne   D. Rosacea

19.____

20. A _____ is defined as a plugged sebaceous gland with an opening that is not widely dilated.
    A. whitehead   B. blackhead   C. furuncle   D. carbuncle

20.____

21. Foul-smelling perspiration caused by the yeast and bacteria that break down the sweat on the surface of the skin is referred to as
    A. anhidrosis   B. hyperhidrosis
    C. bromhidrosis   D. fungihidrosis

21.____

22. Eccrine glands are primarily responsible for which of the following processes?
    A. Sebum secretion   B. Collagen production
    C. Thermoregulation   D. Hormone regulation

22.____

23. Which acid promotes skin drying and cell turnover?
    A. Azaleic   B. Glycolic   C. Salicylic   D. Hyaluronic

23.____

24. According to the Fitzpatrick prototype scale, what skin type almost always burns and tans minimally?
    A. Type 1   B. Type 2   C. Type 3   D. Type 4

24.____

25. Which medical condition, as illustrated in the image shown at the right, is commonly referred to as baby acne?
    A. Milia
    B. Rosacea
    C. Lentigo
    D. Nevus

25.____

KEY (CORRECT ANSWERS)

1.	A		11.	D
2.	A		12.	D
3.	D		13.	D
4.	B		14.	C
5.	C		15.	D
6.	D		16.	A
7.	B		17.	B
8.	C		18.	C
9.	B		19.	A
10.	A		20.	A

21. C
22. C
23. A
24. B
25. A

TEST 3

DIRECTIONS: Each question or incomplete statement is followed by several suggested answers or completions. Select the one that BEST answers the question or completes the statement. *PRINT THE LETTER OF THE CORRECT ANSWER IN THE SPACE AT THE RIGHT.*

1. Hair is primarily composed of what substance? 1.____
   A. Keratin   B. Collagen   C. Albumin   D. Magnesium

2. Which of the following is defined as a tube-like depression in the skin that encases the hair root? 2.____
   A. Bulb   B. Papilla   C. Follicle   D. Arrector pili

3. Which of the following refers to the club-shaped structure that forms the lower part of the hair root? 3.____
   A. Bulb   B. Papilla   C. Follicle   D. Arrector pili

4. The innermost layer of the hair is referred to as the pith marrow or 4.____
   A. cortex   B. cuticle   C. medulla   D. follicle

5. The growing phase of hair growth is referred to as which of the following? 5.____
   A. Biogen   B. Anagen   C. Telogen   D. Catagen

6. The transitional phase of hair growth is referred to as which of the following? 6.____
   A. Biogen   B. Anagen   C. Telogen   D. Catagen

7. The resting phase of the hair growth cycles is referred to as which of the following? 7.____
   A. Biogen   B. Anagen   C. Telogen   D. Catagen

8. Which of the following is defined as the hair's ability to absorb moisture? 8.____
   A. Density   B. Elasticity   C. Porosity   D. Viscosity

9. Scientists believe that approximately 95% of hair loss is caused by what progressive condition? 9.____
   A. Alopecia totalis   B. Alopecia areata
   C. Alopecia universalis   D. Androgenetic alopecia

10. Alopecia areata is defined as 10.____
    A. slow baldness
    B. male pattern baldness
    C. sudden hair loss in round or irregular patches
    D. hair loss due to repetitive pulling or twisted

11. When testing for telogen effluvium, the client is said to have active shedding if more than how many hairs come out? 11.____
    A. 1-3   B. 3-5   C. 5-10   D. 10-20

2 (#3)

12. What topical solution can be applied to the scalp that has been medically proven to regrow hair?
    A. Follicidil   B. Minoxidil   C. Finasteride   D. Methacrylate

12.____

13. Hair is made up of what five elements?
Carbon, nitrogen, hydrogen,
    A. oxygen, and sulfur   B. copper, and oxygen
    C. oxygen, and sodium   D. sulfur, and chlorine

13.____

14. The color of hair is generally related to which of the following?
    A. Texture of hair   B. Porosity of hair
    C. Health of the hair   D. Number of hairs on the head

14.____

15. Among the various natural hair colors, what color is generally the thickest and has the highest density?
    A. Red   B. Black   C. Brown   D. Blonde

15.____

16. At any one time, approximately what percentage of hair is in the anagen phase?
    A. 60%   B. 70%   C. 80%   D. 90%

16.____

17. Canities is the technical term for which of the following?
    A. Gray hair   B. Dandruff
    C. Beaded hair   D. Brittle hair

17.____

18. Which of the following refers to a prescription medication that is taken orally for the treatment of androgenetic alopecia?
    A. Follicidil   B. Minoxidil   C. Finasteride   D. Methacrylate

18.____

19. What medical condition, as illustrated in the image shown at the right, is characterized by dry, sulfur-yellow, cuplike crusts on the scalp?
    A. Tinea capitis
    B. Tinea favosa
    C. Pityriasis steatoides
    C. Pityriasis capitis simplex

19.____

20. What medical conditions, as illustrated in the image shown at the right, is characterized by greasy or waxy dandruff?
    A. Tinea capitis
    B. Tinea favosa
    C. Pityriasis steatoides
    D. Pityriasis capitis simplex

20.____

21. What medical condition, as illustrated in the image shown at the right, is characterized by dry dandruff?
    A. Tinea capitis
    B. Tinea favosa
    C. Pityriasis steatoides
    D. Pityriasis capitis simplex

21.____

22. Which of the following refers to hairs that may split at any part of their length?
    A. Pityriasis
    B. Monilethrix
    C. Trichoptilosis
    D. Fragilitas crinium

22.____

23. A furuncle is an acute, localized bacterial infection of which of the following?
    A. Sweat pore
    B. Sebaceous gland
    C. Hair follicle
    D. Sudoriferous gland

23.____

24. Inflammation of the subcutaneous tissue, known as a carbuncle, is generally caused by what form of bacteria?
    A. Legionnaires
    B. Salmonella
    C. Staphylococcus
    D. Cryptosporidium

24.____

25. What medical condition, as illustrated in the image shown at the right, is a contagious skin disease caused by the itch mite?
    A. Carbuncle
    B. Scabies
    C. Ringworm
    D. Tinea capitis

25.____

KEY (CORRECT ANSWERS)

1.	A	11.	B
2.	C	12.	B
3.	A	13.	A
4.	C	14.	D
5.	B	15.	D
6.	D	16.	D
7.	C	17.	A
8.	C	18.	C
9.	D	19.	B
10.	C	20.	C

21. D
22. D
23. C
24. C
25. B

TEST 4

DIRECTIONS: Each question or incomplete statement is followed by several suggested answers or completions. Select the one that BEST answers the question or completes the statement. *PRINT THE LETTER OF THE CORRECT ANSWER IN THE SPACE AT THE RIGHT.*

1. Small follicles are indicative of what type of skin? 1.____
   A. Dry B. Oily C. Normal D. Combination

2. What skin type has an unhealthy acid mantle and skin barrier function? 2.____
   A. Dry B. Oily C. Normal D. Combination

3. Follicles going from smaller to medium just on the edge of the T-zone by the nose is characteristic of what skin type? 3.____
   A. Dry B. Oily C. Normal D. Combination

4. Skin that lacks oxygen is referred to as what type of skin? 4.____
   A. Dry B. Oily C. Combination D. Asphyxiated

5. Touching the skin with your fingers during a skin analysis helps to determine whether or not the skin is 5.____
   A. dry B. oily C. rough D. dehydrated

6. Which of the following describes skin damage or a skin condition caused by sun exposure? 6.____
   A. Actinic B. Alipidic C. Lipophilic D. Lipophobic

7. Which of the following describes skin that does not produce enough sebum, indicated by the absence of visible pores? 7.____
   A. Actinic B. Alipidic C. Lipophilic D. Lipophobic

8. Which of the following is a condition in which the skin appears red due to the presence of small, dilated, red blood vessels visible on the face? 8.____
   A. Combination skin B. Couperose skin
   C. Rosacea D. Erythema

9. Wrinkling as a result of photodamage and the aging process is measured according to which of the following? 9.____
   A. Fitzpatrick scale B. Glogau scale
   C. Rubin classification D. Monheit and Fulton system

10. What is used to measure the skin's ability to tolerate sun exposure? 10.____
    A. Fitzpatrick scale B. Glogau scale
    C. Rubin classification D. Monheit and Fulton system

11. Which of the following is used to classify photodamage by the depth of skin changes or damage?
    A. Fitzpatrick scale
    B. Glogau scale
    C. Rubin classification
    D. Monheit and Fulton system

12. For what reason are occlusive products used?
    A. Reduce pore clogging
    B. Reduce oil loss
    C. Reduce water loss
    D. Increase sebum production

13. What skin condition, as illustrated in the image shown at the right, is characterized by skin redness as a result of inflammation?
    A. Combination skin
    B. Couperose skin
    C. Rosacea
    D. Erythema

14. Approximately what percentage of water is found in healthy skin?
    A. 30-40%
    B. 40-50%
    C. 50-70%
    D. 70-80%

15. What medical condition, as illustrated in the image shown at the right, is characterized by a bacterial infection of the hairy parts of the face and neck?
    A. Sycosis
    B. Impetigo
    C. Furunculosis
    D. Herpes Zoster

16. Which of the following is defined as baldness due to scarring of the skin by chemical or physical means in which the hair follicle is permanently damaged and there is no treatment?
    A. Alopecia totalis
    B. Alopecia universalis
    C. Cicatrical alopecia
    D. Traction alopecia

17. _____ is a naturally occurring fungus that lives on the human skin and causes dandruff.
    A. Aspergillus
    B. Fusarium
    C. Cryptococcus
    D. Malassezia

18. Which of the following would be considered to be an internal factor causing dandruff? 18.____
    A. Hormonal imbalance
    B. Lack of proper cleansing
    C. Infrequent shampooing
    D. Increased activity of bacteria or fungi

19. Which of the following would be considered to be an external factor causing dandruff? 19.____
    A. Stress and tension   B. Poor nutrition
    C. Poor scalp stimulation D. Glandular problems

20. A crack in the skin that penetrates to the dermis is referred to as a(n) 20.____
    A. abrasion   B. laceration   C. fissure   D. puncture

21. In order for chemicals to penetrate a healthy cuticle layer, they must have which of the following? 21.____
    A. Low pH   B. Acidic pH   C. Neutral pH   D. Alkalkine pH

22. Of the 20 twenty amino acids required for hair production, how many can the human body actually produce? 22.____
    A. 6   B. 11   C. 15   D. 19

23. What type of chemical bond accounts for about one-third of the hair's overall strength? 23.____
    A. Hydrogen   B. Peptide   C. Salt   D. Disulfide

24. What type of chemical bond holds the chains of amino acids together and the position of these bonds determines the curl that is present in the hair? 24.____
    A. Hydrogen   B. Peptide   C. Salt   D. Sulfur

25. What type of chemical bond can be easily broken by weak alkaline or acidic solutions and changes in pH, however, can be reformed by normalizing the pH level of the hair? 25.____
    A. Hydrogen   B. Peptide   C. Salt   D. Sulfur

KEY (CORRECT ANSWERS)

1. A
2. A
3. C
4. D
5. C

6. A
7. B
8. B
9. B
10. A

11. C
12. C
13. D
14. C
15. A

16. C
17. D
18. A
19. C
20. C

21. D
22. B
23. A
24. D
25. C

SKIN & HAIR

EXAMINATION SECTION
TEST 1

DIRECTIONS: Each question consists of a statement. You are to indicate whether the statement is TRUE (T) or FALSE (F). *PRINT THE LETTER OF THE CORRECT ANSWER IN THE SPACE AT THE RIGHT.*

1. Heat contracts and cold dilates the skin.   1____
2. The subcutaneous layer of the skin lies directly beneath the corium.   2____
3. Corium, derma, and true skin are the same.   3____
4. The skin is an external non-flexible covering of the body.   4____
5. Dermatology is the study of the hair.   5____
6. The skin is an organ of elimination.   6____
7. The appendages of the skin are the nails, hair, sebaceous and sudoriferous glands.   7____
8. Skin absorbs water readily.   8____
9. Health, age, and occupation have no influence on the texture of the skin.   9____
10. Elimination is an important function of the skin.   10____
11. The skin is the organ of protection, absorption, elimination, heat regulation, respiration, and sensation.   11____
12. Age has no effect on the elasticity of the skin.   12____
13. The skin is the seat of the organ of touch.   13____
14. The sebaceous glands secrete an oily substance called sebum.   14____
15. The skin is the same thickness over the entire body.   15____
16. Hair is an appendage of the nails.   16____
17. Keratin is the horny substance of which hair is made.   17____
18. The amount of pigment contained in the cortex determines the color of hair.   18____
19. The blood vessels which nourish the hair are located in the hair papillae.   19____
20. When the blood supply is cut off, the growth of hair is stopped.   20____
21. Under normal conditions, hair grows about one-half inch a month.   21____
22. Hair does not act as a protection.   22____

23. Hair will grow again even though the papilla has been destroyed.   23____

24. The life of an eyelash is from four to five months.   24____

25. There are more hairs than follicles.   25____

26. After a hair has fallen out, a new hair will appear in about ten days.   26____

27. Hair has no blood vessels.   27____

28. The average life of a hair is from six to eight years.   28____

29. Canities can be cured by scalp treatments.   29____

30. The health of the hair depends on the health of the body.   30____

KEY (CORRECT ANSWERS)

1.	F	11.	T	21.	T
2.	T	12.	F	22.	F
3.	T	13.	T	23.	F
4.	F	14.	T	24.	T
5.	F	15.	F	25.	F
6.	T	16.	F	26.	F
7.	T	17.	T	27.	T
8.	F	18.	T	28.	F
9.	F	19.	T	29.	F
10.	T	20.	T	30.	T

TEST 2

DIRECTIONS: Each question consists of a statement. You are to indicate whether the statement is TRUE (T) or FALSE (F). *PRINT THE LETTER OF THE CORRECT ANSWER IN THE SPACE AT THE RIGHT.*

1. Acne is the most common skin disorder encountered in beauty shops.   1____
2. Trichophytosis is the term applied to ringworm of the scalp.   2____
3. Carbuncles are caused by a germ.   3____
4. Anthrax may be treated by a beautician.   4____
5. Regular alopecia treatments alternated with hot oil treatments will correct canities.   5____
6. Scabies refers to head lice.   6____
7. Tinea tonsurans is ringworm of the scalp.   7____
8. Keloid is a wartlike growth commonly located in the eyelids.   8____
9. A communicable disease is one that can be transmitted from person to person.   9____
10. Alopecia areata is baldness at time of birth.   10____
11. Pityriasis is the term applied to an excessively oily condition of the scalp.   11____
12. Keratosis is a form of skin disease characterized by thinning epidermis.   12____
13. An acute disease is one of long duration.   13____
14. Canities is caused by fever, shock, nervousness, or senility.   14____
15. Eczema is a contagious, parasitic disease of the skin, with crust formations, emitting a mousy odor.   15____
16. Scalp hair is known as hypertrichosis.   16____
17. Dermatitis venenata is the technical name for dye poisoning.   17____
18. Trichorrhexis nodosa is the technical name for matted hair and can be treated with oil and vinegar.   18____
19. Scars, ulcers, and fissures are known as secondary lesions.   19____
20. Favus is not a disease of the hair, but of the hair follicle, and can be recognized by being gray in color, cup-like in shape, and having a mousy odor.   20____
21. Symptoms of alopecia areata and alopecia senilis are the same.   21____
22. Brushing is avoided in treatments for an oily scalp.   22____
23. Pediculosis capitis is a scaly condition of the scalp.   23____
24. Hair has no blood vessels.   24____

25. A tight scalp is favorable to the growth of hair. 25____
26. The cause of eczema is unknown. 26____
27. Water is absorbed through the skin; oils and ointments are not. 27____
28. Eczema may be either an acute or chronic inflammation. 28____
29. The skin cannot function properly if the pores are clogged with dust, creams, or sebum. 29____
30. If the skin has a tendency to be very dry, soap should be used regularly. 30____
31. Erysipelas is an acute inflammation of the skin. 31____
32. The technical name for freckle is lentigo. 32____
33. Impetigo is not contagious. 33____
34. Sebum keeps the skin lubricated and pliable. 34____
35. Favus is a form of ringworm. 35____
36. Ringworm is a non-contagious disease. 36____
37. Erythema is a blue condition of the skin. 37____
38. Pityriasis is the presence of white scales in the hair and scalp. 38____
39. Pityriasis is the technical name for dandruff. 39____
40. The symptoms of pityriasis capitis are itching scalp, dry dandruff, and a partial loss of hair. 40____
41. Certain ingredients in cosmetics may cause a dermatitis. 41____
42. Hot packs are recommended for acne rosacea treatments. 42____
43. Dandruff is considered a disease if the shedding of scales is excessive. 43____
44. An albino is a person with an abnormal deficiency of pigment in the skin, hair, and eyes. 44____
45. Oily foods tend to aggravate a dry condition of the skin. 45____
46. Objective symptoms are visible and hence can be treated by a beautician. 46____
47. Acne rosacea affects the sweat glands. 47____
48. A macule is the same as a freckle. 48____
49. Anidrosis means the same as excessive perspiration. 49____
50. Fatty foods give the skin a sheen. 50____

KEY (CORRECT ANSWERS)

1. T	11. F	21. F	31. T	41. T
2. T	12. F	22. T	32. T	42. F
3. T	13. F	23. F	33. F	43. T
4. F	14. T	24. T	34. T	44. T
5. F	15. F	25. F	35. T	45. F
6. F	16. F	26. T	36. F	46. F
7. T	17. T	27. F	37. F	47. F
8. F	18. F	28. T	38. T	48. T
9. T	19. T	29. T	39. T	49. F
10. F	20. T	30. F	40. T	50. F

TEST 3

DIRECTIONS: Fill in the blanks with the MOST appropriate word from the set of words at the beginning of each section. Each answer may be used only once.

Questions 1-10.

corneum	water	corium	98.6
pliable	face	dermis	pigment
cuticle	tactile	tubular	sacular

1. The two main divisions of the skin are the epidermis or _____ and the dermis or _____ .

2. Scale-like cells which flake off are found in the stratum

3. The elastic cells of the dermis make the skin _____.

4. Papillae containing nerve fibres are called corpuscles.

5. Subcutaneous tissue is found below the _____.

6. The sweat glands are simple _____ glands and the oil glands are of the _____ type.

7. The color of the skin depends upon its blood supply and _____ content.

8. The skin regulates the temperature of the body to about _____ degrees Fahrenheit.

9. Oil glands are most numerous upon the.

10. Perspiration consists mainly of _____.

Questions 11-20.

sebum	blood	coarse	sebaceous
20	cold	silky	medulla
lips	short	scalp	bristly
fear	cortex	white	cuticle

11. No hair is found on the palms, soles, and _____.

12. Soft, long hair grows under the armpits and on the _____.

13. The eyebrows and eyelashes have _____ or _____ hair.

14. The three layers of the hair are the medulla, _____ , and _____.

15. The source of pigment in the hair is probably derived from color-forming substances in the _____ .

16. Air spaces and a lack of pigment makes the hair appear _____.

17. The arrector pilli muscle contracts because of _____ or _____.

18. Normal hair will stretch _____ percent of its natural length.

19. The _____ glands empty an oily substance at the mouth of the hair follicle called _____ .

20. The operator should be able to differentiate between fine and _____, or wiry and _____ hair texture.

Questions 21-30.

parasitic	papule	pus	epidermis
chronic	disease	birth	circulatory
pimple	vesicle	bulla	deficiency

21. A yellow-green crust present in a skin disease is indicative of dried _____ .

22. A congenital disease is present at the time of _____ .

23. Primary skin lesions containing a serum-like fluid are _____ and _____ .

24. A scale is a separated portion of the _____ .

25. The opposite of health is _____ .

26. Neglect to take care of an acute disease may result in the development of a _____ disease.

27. A constitutional disease spreads all over the body by way of the _____ system.

28. A _____ disease is due to the lack of an important element in the diet.

29. Scabies and ringworm are examples of _____ diseases.

30. A skin eruption common to adolescents is called a _____ .

Questions 31-40.

papules	pits	comedones	milia
blackheads	face	lesions	nose
pustules	scars	digestive	dry
seborrhea	cyst	alkalies	tumor

31. Whiteheads are called _____ , and blackheads are known as

32. Comedones appear most frequently on the _____ and _____ .

33. The skin lesions present in acne rosacea are _____ and _____ .

34. A sign of asteatosis is a _____ skin.

35. A local condition of asteatosis may be caused by _____ in soaps.

36. Steatoma is a sebaceous _____ or _____ .

37. An oily and shiny condition of the scalp, nose, and forehead is an indication of _____ .

38. Disturbances of the _____ system is a contributory cause of acne.

39. The healing of skin lesions in acute hypertrophica may result in the formation of conspicuous _____ and _____ .

40. Abnormal changes in skin tissue formation are known as a _____ .

KEY (CORRECT ANSWERS)

1. cuticle, corium
2. corneum
3. pliable
4. tactile
5. dermis
6. tubular, sacular
7. pigment
8. 98.6
9. face
10. water
11. lips
12. scalp
13. short, bristly
14. cortex, cuticle
15. blood
16. white
17. fear, cold
18. 20
19. sebaceous, sebum
20. coarse, silky
21. pus
22. birth
23. bulla, vesicle
24. epidermis
25. disease
26. chronic
27. circulatory
28. deficiency
29. parasitic
30. pimple
31. milia, comedones
32. face, nose
33. papules, pustules
34. dry
35. alkalies
36. cyst, tumor
37. seborrhea
38. digestive
39. pits, scars
40. lesions

TEST 4

DIRECTIONS: In each set of questions, match the descriptions in Column *II* with the appropriate item in Column I. *PRINT THE LETTER OF THE CORRECT ANSWER IN THE SPACE AT THE RIGHT.*

Questions 1-6. Skin Lesions.

COLUMN I

1. Fissure
2. Papule
3. Tumor
4. Ulcer
5. Pustule
6. Scar

COLUMN II.

A. Open skin lesion having pus
B. Healed wound or ulcer
C. Inflamed elevation of the skin having pus
D. Pimple
E. Deep crack in the skin
F. External swelling

1._____
2._____
3._____
4._____
5._____
6._____

Questions 7-11.   Forms of Acne.

7. Acne papulosa
8. Acne punctata
9. Acne induBrata
10. Acne rosacea
11. Acne pustulosa

A. Deep-seated hardened lesion
B. Congestion of the skin
C. Inflamed pimples
D. Pimples containing pus
E. Red papules containing blackheads

7._____
8._____
9._____
10._____
11._____

Questions 12-17.   Diseases.

12. Anidrosis
13. Hyperidrosis
14. Miliary fever
15. Bromidrosis
16. Chromidrosis
17. Miliaria rubra

A. Foul smelling perspiration
B. Prickly heat
C. Discolored perspiration
D. Lack of perspiration
E. Sweating sickness
F. Excessive perspiration

12._____
13._____
14._____
15._____
16._____
17._____

Questions 18-24.   Diseases.

18. Canities
19. Dermatitis

A. Dandruff
B. Dry type of dandruff

18._____
19._____

COLUMN I	COLUMN II	
20. Urticaria	C. Oily type of dandruff	20.____
21. Pityriasis steatoides	D. Grey hair	21.____
22. Pityriasis capitis	E. Inflammation of the skin	22.____
23. Furuncle	F. Eruption of itching wheals	23.____
24. Pityriasis	G. Boil	24.____

Questions 25-31.   Diseases.

25. Psoriasis	A. Large boil	25.____
26. Syphilis	B. Vesicles resting on an inflamed base	26.____
27. Eczema	C. Malignant pustule	27.____
28. Carbuncle	D. Patches of dry, white scales	28.____
29. Pityriasis pilaris	D. Dry or moist lesions	29.____
30. Herpes simplex	E. Papules, pustules, tubercles, and ulcerations	30.____
31. Anthrax	F. Papules surrounding the hair follicles	31.____

Questions 32-38.   Diseases.

32. Alopecia adnata	A. Ringworm of the scalp	32.____
33. Fragilitas crinium	B. Baldness in spots	33.____
34. Monilethrix	C. Head louse	34.____
35. Alopecia areata	D. Congenital baldness	35.____
36. Trichoptilosis	E. Beaded hair	36.____
37. Trichophytosis	F. Brittle hair	37.____
38. Pediculosis capitis	G. Split hair	38.____

Questions 39-45.   Diseases.

39. Hypertrophy	A. Congenital absence of pigment in the body	39.____
40. Albinism	A. Malignant skin cancer	40.____
41. Chloasma	C. Abnormal growth of an organ	41.____

42. Epithelioma	D. Defective skin pigmentation	42.____
43. Leucoderma	E. Increased skin pigmentation	43.____
44. Trachoma	F. Granulated eyelids	44.____
45. Atrophy	G. Abnormal wasting of an organ or structure	45.____

KEY (CORRECT ANSWERS)

1. E	11. D	21. C	31. C	41. E
2. D	12. D	22. B	32. D	42. B
3. F	13. F	23. G	33. F	43. D
4. A	14. E	24. A	34. E	44. F
5. C	15. A	25. D	35. B	45. G
6. B	16. C	26. F	36. G	
7. C	17. B	27. E	37. A	
8. E	18. D	28. A	38. C	
9. A	19. E	29. G	39. C	
10. B	20. F	30. B	40. A	

EXAMINATION SECTION
TEST 1

DIRECTIONS: Each question or incomplete statement is followed by several suggested answers or completions. Select the one that BEST answers the question or completes the statement. *PRINT THE LETTER OF THE CORRECT ANSWER IN THE SPACE AT THE RIGHT.*

1. Which of the following is defined as the study of hair?
   A. Trichology
   B. Onychology
   C. Dermatology
   D. Epidemiology

   1.____

2. Which of the following represent the chief purposes of hair?
   A. Oil reduction and protection
   B. Adornment and sweat diversion
   C. Adornment and protection
   D. Sweat diversion and protection

   2.____

3. _____ is the technical term for eyelash hair.
   A. Cilia
   B. Barba
   C. Capilli
   D. Flagella

   3.____

4. Hair is composed primarily of what substance?
   A. Collagen
   B. Keratin
   C. Melanin
   D. Glycogen

   4.____

5. The chemical composition of hair varies with which of the following?
   A. Hair color
   B. Hair thickness
   C. Hair length
   D. Hair growth pattern

   5.____

6. Which of the following is the MOST prominent type of hair on the human body?
   A. Cilia
   B. Lanugo
   C. Vellus hair
   D. Terminal hair

   6.____

7. At a right angle to the direction of hair growth, an imaginary line known as the Line of _____ separates the follicle bulb at the widest part of the papilla into an upper and lower region.
   A. Auber
   B. Symmetry
   C. Proportion
   D. Demarcation

   7.____

8. What type of hair is thick, may have a medulla, can vary in length, and is primarily found on the head or face?
   A. Cilia
   B. Lanugo
   C. Vellus hair
   D. Terminal hair

   8.____

9. Which of the following represents the two main divisions of the hair?
   A. Bulb and follicle
   B. Hair root and papilla
   C. Hair root and hair shaft
   D. Hair shaft and follicle

   9.____

10. In what region is the hair root located?   10.____
    A. Within the cortex   B. Under the cuticle
    C. Above the skin surface   D. Below the skin surface

11. Which of the following represents the three main structures associated   11.____
    with the hair root?
    A. Follicle, bulb, and papilla   B. Follicle, bulb, and medulla
    C. Follicle, bulb, and matrix   D. Follicle, papilla, and medulla

12. What structure is a tube-like depression in the skin that encases the hair   12.____
    root?
    A. Bulb   B. Papilla   C. Follicle   D. Medulla

13. Which of the following is the club-shaped structure that forms the lower   13.____
    part of the hair root?
    A. Bulb   B. Papilla   C. Follicle   D. Medulla

14. In what region is the papilla located?   14.____
    A. Above the hair root   B. Below the medulla
    C. At the skin surface   D. At the bottom of the follicle

15. Which of the following is defined as the small involuntary muscle that is   15.____
    attached to the underside of the follicle?
    A. Epicranius   B. Arrector pili
    C. Tendinous aponeurosis   D. Galea aponeurotica

16. Which of the following glands are commonly referred to as oil glands?   16.____
    A. Apocrine   B. Endocrine   C. Sebaceous   D. Sudoriferous

17. The sebaceous glands secrete an oily substance referred to as   17.____
    A. serum   B. sebum   C. plasma   D. sweat

18. To what are sebaceous glands connected?   18.____
    A. Dermis   B. Epidermis   C. Hair roots   D. Hair follicles

19. Which of the following represents the three layers of hair?   19.____
    A. Cuticle, cortex, and bulb   B. Cuticle, root, and medulla
    C. Cuticle, cortex, and medulla   D. Cuticle, bulb, and medulla

20. The scale-like cells of the cuticle protect what region?   20.____
    A. Root   B. Scalp
    C. Outside horny layer   D. Inner structure of the hair

21. The hair pigment is found in what layer?   21.____
    A. Cortex   B. Cuticle   C. Medulla   D. Papilla

22. The innermost layer of the hair is referred to as the _____, or medulla.   22.____
    A. cortex   B. cuticle
    C. pitch marrow   D. protective layer

23. Which of the following statements is TRUE regarding the papilla? 23.____
    If the papilla is destroyed, the hair will
    A. regrow
    B. grow back gray
    C. grow in thicker
    D. never grow again

24. How often are eyebrows and eyelashes replaced? 24.____
    A. Daily
    B. Weekly
    C. Monthly
    D. Every 4-5 months

25. The strength, texture, and natural color of hair is primarily dependent upon 25.____
    which of the following?
    A. Heredity
    B. Diet
    C. Exposure to sunlight
    D. pH of hair care products

KEY (CORRECT ANSWERS)

1.	A		11.	A
2.	C		12.	C
3.	A		13.	A
4.	B		14.	D
5.	A		15.	B
6.	C		16.	C
7.	A		17.	B
8.	C		18.	D
9.	C		19.	C
10.	D		20.	D

21. A
22. C
23. D
24. D
25. A

TEST 2

DIRECTIONS: Each question or incomplete statement is followed by several suggested answers or completions. Select the one that BEST answers the question or completes the statement. *PRINT THE LETTER OF THE CORRECT ANSWER IN THE SPACE AT THE RIGHT.*

1. As illustrated in the image shown at the right, which of the following is a condition in which a person is born with an absence of coloring matter in the hair shaft and no marked pigment coloring in the skin or irises of the eye?
    A. Vitiligo
    B. Lanugo
    C. Albinism
    D. Melanism

    1._____

2. Which of the following statements is TRUE regarding gray hair? Gray hair
    A. sheds easily
    B. forms in response to age
    C. forms in response to stress
    D. grows that way from the bulb

    2._____

3. What is the PRIMARY cause of gray hair?
    A. Vitamin deficiency
    B. Stress
    C. Normal aging process
    D. Chronic medical condition

    3._____

4. Which of the following statements is TRUE regarding vellus hair? Vellus hair is
    A. curly
    B. coarse
    C. pigmented
    D. non-pigmented

    4._____

5. Which of the following represents the three phases of hair growth?
    A. Anagen, catagen, biogen
    B. Anagen, biogen, telogen
    C. Catagen, biogen, telogen
    D. Anagen, catagen, telogen

    5._____

6. Which of the following is known as the growing phase of hair growth?
    A. Biogen
    B. Anagen
    C. Catogen
    D. Telogen

    6._____

7. Which of the following is known as the transitional phase of hair growth?
    A. Biogen
    B. Anagen
    C. Catogen
    D. Telogen

    7._____

8. Hair continues to grow for what period of time?
    A. 3-6 months
    B. 6-12 months
    C. 1-2 years
    D. 2-6 years

    8._____

9. The transitional phase of hair growth lasts for what period of time?
    A. 1-2 days
    B. 3-5 days
    C. 5-7 days
    D. 1-2 weeks

    9._____

10. Which of the following statements is TRUE regarding the follicle during catagen?
    During catagen, the follicle
    A. thickens
    B. lengthens
    C. decreases in volume
    D. increases in volume

    10.____

11. The lower part of what structure is destroyed during the transitional phase of the hair life cycle?
    A. Papilla
    B. Hair root
    C. Hair bulb
    D. Hair follicle

    11.____

12. Which of the following is known as the resting phase of hair growth?
    A. Biogen
    B. Anagen
    C. Catogen
    D. Telogen

    12.____

13. As illustrated in the image shown at the right, a whorl is formed when hair grows in what pattern?
    A. Tuft
    B. Circular
    C. Clockwise
    D. Conflicting

    13.____

14. As illustrated in the image shown at the right, what is formed when a tuft of hair is standing up?
    A. Whirl
    B. Cowlick
    C. Curl
    D. Point

    14.____

15. Which of the following represents the three hair shapes?
    A. Round, oval, and spherical
    B. Round, spherical, and concentric
    C. Round, oval, and almost flat
    D. Round, spherical, and almost flat

    15.____

16. If a person has straight hair, the hair itself is in what shape?
    A. Round
    B. Oval
    C. Almost flat
    D. Spherical

    16.____

17. Which of the following determines the shape of hair a person will have?
    A. A person's diet
    B. A person's nationality
    C. The size of the hair root
    D. The direction of hair as it projects out of the follicle

    17._____

18. The degree of coarseness or fineness of hair refers to the hair
    A. texture   B. porosity   C. elasticity   D. density

    18._____

19. What type of hair has the GREATEST diameter?
    A. Fine   B. Coarse   C. Thick   D. Gray

    19._____

20. _____ refers to the hair's ability to absorb moisture.
    A. Texture   B. Porosity   C. Elasticity   D. Density

    20._____

21. _____ refers to the ability of the hair to stretch and return to its normal form without breaking.
    A. Texture   B. Porosity   C. Elasticity   D. Density

    21._____

22. For hair with _____, it may take a longer amount of time for chemicals to penetrate hair.
    A. fine texture
    B. medium texture
    C. good porosity
    D. poor porosity

    22._____

23. A miniaturization of certain scalp follicles contributes to what condition?
    A. Alopecia areata
    B. Telogen effluvium
    C. Postpartum alopecia
    D. Androgenetic alopecia

    23._____

24. The hair loss process is a gradual conversion of terminal hair follicles to which of the following?
    A. Lanugo-like follicles
    B. Vellum-like follicles
    C. Dome-shaped follicles
    D. Horseshoe-shaped follicles

    24._____

25. Which of the following statements is TRUE regarding androgenetic alopecia? Androgenetic alopecia
    A. alters follicle structure
    B. increases follicle numbers
    C. does not change follicle size
    D. does not alter the number of follicles

    25._____

KEY (CORRECT ANSWERS)

1. C
2. D
3. C
4. D
5. D

6. B
7. C
8. D
9. D
10. C

11. D
12. D
13. B
14. B
15. C

16. A
17. D
18. A
19. B
20. B

21. C
22. D
23. D
24. B
25. D

TEST 3

DIRECTIONS: Each question or incomplete statement is followed by several suggested answers or completions. Select the one that BEST answers the question or completes the statement. *PRINT THE LETTER OF THE CORRECT ANSWER IN THE SPACE AT THE RIGHT.*

1. As illustrated in the image shown at the right, alopecia areata is defined as
   A. male pattern baldness
   B. baldness due to chronic medical condition
   C. sudden hair loss in round or irregular patches
   D. hair loss due to repetitive pulling or twisting of hair

   1.____

   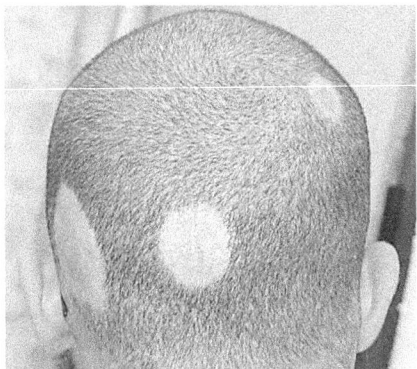

2. Which of the following statements is TRUE regarding telogen effluvium? Telogen effluvium
   A. is incurable
   B. is hereditary
   C. can be reversed
   D. only affects men

   2.____

3. As illustrated in the image shown at the right, excessive application of chemicals or excessive use of hot combs can lead to what condition?
   A. Androgenetic alopecia
   B. Alopecia areata
   C. Traumatic alopecia
   D. Traction alopecia

   3.____

   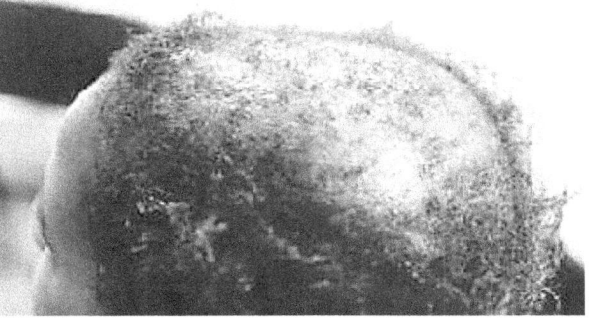

4. In what manner can a cosmetologist recognize miniaturized hairs on a client's scalp?
   Hair has _____ ends.
   A. flat   B. split   C. pointed   D. rounded

   4.____

5. What is an easy way to recognize androgenetic alopecia among females?
   A. A widening hair part
   B. Horseshoe-shaped balding pattern
   C. Fuller diameter ponytail
   D. Smaller diameter ponytail

   5.____

6. The degree of hair loss in men can be evaluated by rating which of the following?
   A. Pattern and density
   B. Pattern and texture
   C. Texture and density
   D. Texture and elasticity

7. Regarding male pattern baldness, the scalp is divided into what three regions?
   A. Front, mid-area, and apex
   B. Front, apex, and vertex
   C. Front, mid-area, and vertex
   D. Front, vertex, and parietal

8. As illustrated in the image shown at the right, which of the following is a condition characterized by an abnormal development of hair on areas of the body that normally only contain vellus hair?
   A. Hyperhidrosis
   B. Hypertrichosis
   C. Monilethrix
   D. Fragilitas cranium

9. Which of the following is the technical term for "split ends"?
   A. Monilethrix
   B. Hyperhidrosis
   C. Hypertrichosis
   D. Trichoptilosis

10. As illustrated in the image shown at the right, what condition is identified by nodular swellings along the hair shaft?
    A. Trichorrhexis
    B. Trichoptilosis
    C. Monolethrix
    D. Hypertrichosis

11. As illustrated in the picture shown at the right, which of the following is an autosomal disorder characterized by a beaded appearance of the hair due to periodic thinning of the shaft?
    A. Trichorrhexis
    B. Trichoptilosis
    C. Monolethrix
    D. Hypertrichosis

12. Which of the following is characterized by brittle hair?
    A. Hyperhidrosis   B. Hypertrichosis
    C. Monilethrix   D. Fragilitas cranium

    12._____

13. The medical term for dandruff is
    A. trichorrhexis   B. trichoptilosis
    C. monolethrix   D. pityriasis

    13._____

14. Tinea is commonly carried by scales or hairs containing which of the following?
    A. Bacteria   B. Viruses   C. Fungi   D. Protozoa

    14._____

15. Tinea is the medical term for
    A. ringworm   B. scabies   C. dandruff   D. psoriasis

    15._____

16. As illustrated in the image shown at the right, which of the following conditions is caused by head lice?
    A. Pityriasis
    B. Pediculosis
    C. Monilethrix
    D. Trichorrhexis

    16._____

17. Which of the following are required for a healthy scalp?
    A. Cleanliness and stimulation   B. Cleanliness and conditioning
    C. Conditioning and stimulation   D. Stimulation and treatment

    17._____

18. For a normal scalp, how often should a scalp massage be performed?
    A. Hourly   B. Daily   C. Weekly   D. Monthly

    18._____

19. The mouths of hair follicles are _____ shaped.
    A. tube   B. funnel   C. cylindrical   D. spherical

    19._____

20. Which of the following is responsible for the shine and silkiness of the hair?
    A. Cortex   B. Cuticle   C. Medulla   D. Papilla

    20._____

21. What type of chemical bonds allow the hair to be curled using rollers?
    A. Hydrogen   B. Salt   C. Disulfide   D. Ionic

    21._____

22. Hair that flows in the same direction is referred to as a hair
    A. wave   B. stream   C. current   D. flow

    22._____

23. In order for chemicals to penetrate the healthy cuticle layer, they must have which of the following?
    A. Strongly acidic pH
    B. Mildly acidic pH
    C. Neutral pH
    D. Alkaline pH

24. Which of the following is a process in which living cells mature and begin their journey up the hair shaft?
    A. Osmosis
    B. Mitosis
    C. Meiosis
    D. Trichosis

25. The measurements of individual hair strands on 1 square inch of the scalp is referred to as
    A. texture
    B. porosity
    C. elasticity
    D. density

KEY (CORRECT ANSWERS)

1.	C		11.	C
2.	C		12.	D
3.	C		13.	D
4.	C		14.	C
5.	D		15.	A
6.	A		16.	B
7.	C		17.	A
8.	B		18.	C
9.	D		19.	B
10.	A		20.	B

21.	A
22.	B
23.	D
24.	A
25.	D

TEST 4

DIRECTIONS: Each question or incomplete statement is followed by several suggested answers or completions. Select the one that BEST answers the question or completes the statement. *PRINT THE LETTER OF THE CORRECT ANSWER IN THE SPACE AT THE RIGHT.*

1. Hydrogen chemical relaxers break disulfide bonds and convert them into what type of bonds?
   A. Hydrogen   B. Lanthionine   C. Ionic   D. Covalent

   1.____

2. Scalp massage is contraindicated with clients who have what medical condition?
   A. Diabetes
   B. Fibromyalgia
   C. Severe hypertension
   D. Migraine headaches

   2.____

3. Hair products are classified as either alkaline solution or an acidic solution based on the amount of which of the following?
   A. Hydrogen   B. Oxygen   C. Nitrogen   D. Sulfur

   3.____

4. Red-colored hair contains an iron containing pigment called
   A. anthocyanin
   B. betaxanthin
   C. tricosiderin
   D. astaxanthin

   4.____

5. A scalp treatment should never be performed if which of the following are present on the scalp?
   A. Moles   B. Freckles   C. Vitiligo   D. Abrasions

   5.____

6. What enzyme is a transmembrane protein which is essential to both the synthesis of eumelanin and pheomelanin and is directly linked to hair color?
   A. Tyrosinase
   B. Hydrolase
   C. Isomerase
   D. Oxid-reductase

   6.____

7. During the catagen phase, the hair follicle shrinks to _____ of the normal length.
   A. ½   B. ¼   C. 1/6   D. 1/8

   7.____

8. Which hair structure is only present in large thick hairs?
   A. Medulla   B. Papilla   C. Cortex   D. Cuticle

   8.____

9. Hair grows approximately _____ cm per year and any individual hair is unlikely to grow more than one meter long.
   A. 5   B. 10   C. 15   D. 20

   9.____

10. During the telogen phase, the hair does not grow but stays attached to the follicle while what structure stays in a resting phase below?
    A. Cortex
    B. Medulla
    C. Dermal papilla
    D. Arrector pili muscle

    10.____

11. If a person has wavy hair, the cross-section of the hair would appear
    A. round   B. oval   C. almost flat   D. spherical

12. If a person has curly hair, the cross-section of the hair would appear
    A. round   B. oval   C. almost flat   D. spherical

13. The average hair density is roughly _____ hairs per square inch.
    A. 500   B. 1,700   C. 2,200   D. 3,400

14. Porous hair can easily absorb water because what layer is raised?
    A. Cuticle   B. Cortex   C. Medulla   D. Papilla

15. High-grade proteins such as fish, eggs, cheese, milk, and meat are particularly beneficial because they are rich in what two substances that are essential for healthy hair growth?
    A. Iron and calcium
    B. Nitrogen and sulfur
    C. Magnesium and calcium
    D. Iron and nitrogen

16. What type of blood vessels supply and nourish the papilla?
    A. Arteries   B. Veins   C. Capillaries   D. Arterioles

17. Redheads often look as though they have thick hair because it tends to be of what texture?
    A. Fine   B. Medium   C. Coarse   D. Porous

18. What term has been introduced to identify the hair fiber shedding event as a separate process during hair follicle cycling?
    A. Anagen   B. Catagen   C. Exogen   D. Kenogen

19. Empty hair follicle after shedding of the hair fiber, but before the onset of renewed anagen are in a stage termed
    A. anagen   B. catagen   C. exogen   D. kenogen

20. Hair disorders are fundamentally caused by changes in hair follicle _____ and/or changes to the hair growth cycle.
    A. elasticity   B. porosity   C. texture   D. density

21. As illustrated in the image shown at the right, which of the following is a fungal infection of the hair shaft in which hard nodule made of fungus cling to hair fibers and can cause hair loss?
    A. Folliculitis
    B. Piedra
    C. Pityriasis
    D. Pediculosis

22. As illustrated in the image shown at the right, which of the following is a condition in which hair abruptly falls out in large patches a month or two after a personal shock such as surgery or severe stress?
    A. Alopecia areata
    B. Telogen effluvium
    C. Postpartum alopecia
    D. Androgenetic alopecia

22.____

23. Hirsutism, a condition in which women develop male-pattern hair (facial hair) is usually due to an increase in what hormone?
    A. Estrogen
    B. Progesterone
    C. Testosterone
    D. Aldosterone

23.____

24. Postpartum alopecia, hair loss after delivering a baby, is a form of what condition and usually resolves without treatment?
    A. Alopecia areata
    B. Telogen effluvium
    C. Postpartum alopecia
    D. Androgenetic alopecia

24.____

25. What part of the hair follicle, the short middle section, extends from the insertion of the arrector pili muscle to the entrance of the sebaceous gland duct?
    A. Isthmus
    B. Infundibulum
    C. Bulb
    D. Suprabulb

25.____

KEY (CORRECT ANSWERS)

1. B
2. C
3. A
4. C
5. D

6. A
7. C
8. A
9. B
10. C

11. B
12. C
13. C
14. A
15. B

16. C
17. C
18. C
19. D
20. D

21. B
22. B
23. C
24. B
25. A

EXAMINATION SECTION
TEST 1

DIRECTIONS: Each question or incomplete statement is followed by several suggested answers or completions. Select the one that BEST answers the question or completes the statement. PRINT THE LETTER OF THE CORRECT ANSWER IN THE SPACE AT THE RIGHT.

1. A chemical agent which will prevent the growth of germs is called a(n) 1._____
   A. toxin B. antiseptic C. septic D. astringent

2. Creams should be removed from jars with 2._____
   A. the corner of a towel B. a spatula
   C. the fingers D. a pledget

3. An agent which causes the contraction of living organic tissue and thus checks bleeding is called a(n) 3._____
   A. antiseptic B. disinfectant C. styptic D. glycerine

4. When not in use, sanitized instruments should be kept in 4._____
   A. the pocket B. a dry sanitizer
   C. an insecticide D. a deodorizer

5. Bacteria will be destroyed by 5._____
   A. glycerine B. intense heat
   C. pumice D. freezing

6. Bacteria can enter the body through 6._____
   A. hair B. nails
   C. broken skin D. unbroken skin

7. Instruments which must be sanitized regularly should be made of 7._____
   A. brass B. stainless steel
   C. tin plated copper D. aluminum

8. Pathogenic bacteria create 8._____
   A. immunity B. disease C. anti-toxins D. hormones

9. Milium is the technical name for a 9._____
   A. whitehead B. blackhead C. pimple D. dry skin

10. Pediculosis capitis is the technical term for 10._____
    A. head lice B. itch mites
    C. flies D. mosquitoes

11. Frequent washings with strong soaps may cause the scalp to become   11._____

    A. healthy   B. oily   C. dry   D. flexible

12. The hair and scalp may often be reconditioned with heating cap treatments and   12._____

    A. lemon rinses   B. porosity treatments
    C. scalp massage   D. stripping treatments

13. A tint to which peroxide has been added   13._____

    A. penetrates the hair shaft
    B. gives an orange tone to the hair
    C. coats the hair shaft
    D. lightens the hair

14. A temporary coating of color applied to the hair is called a   14._____

    A. compound dyestuff   B. metallic tint
    C. progressive tint   D. color rinse

15. A penetrating tint is one which penetrates and deposits color permanently into the   15._____

    A. cuticle   B. medulla   C. cortex   D. follicle

16. Hair containing no red or gold tones is known as _____ hair.   16._____

    A. drab   B. lightened
    C. brunette   D. tinted

17. Hair should NEVER be thinned close to the   17._____

    A. sides   B. crown   C. ends   D. scalp

18. The hair should be wet if hairshaping is done with   18._____

    A. shears   B. clippers
    C. razor   D. thinning scissors

19. Thinning the hair involves   19._____

    A. shortening   B. blunt cutting
    C. decreasing its bulk   D. trimming the ends

20. Removal of split hair ends may be accomplished by   20._____

    A. ruffing   B. slithering
    C. blunt cutting   D. feathering

21. Featheredging the neckline is BEST accomplished with   21._____

    A. a coarse toothed comb   B. a lighted wax taper
    C. a razor   D. points of the shears

22. Shortening and thinning the hair at the same time is known as   22._____

    A. clipping   B. ruffing   C. tapering   D. back-combing

23. In basic hair shaping, the length of the strands of hair should NOT vary by more than   23.____

   A. 2 inches   B. 1/4 inch   C. 1 inch   D. 1 1/2 inches

24. Before hair is set, it is important that it be   24.____

   A. shaped   B. clipped   C. ruffed   D. shingled

25. The BEST time to apply scalp manipulations in shampooing is   25.____

   A. before the head has been lathered
   B. after the head has been lathered
   C. after the head has been rinsed
   D. after the head has been dried

KEY (CORRECT ANSWERS)

1.	B	11.	C
2.	B	12.	C
3.	C	13.	A
4.	B	14.	D
5.	B	15.	C
6.	C	16.	A
7.	B	17.	D
8.	B	18.	C
9.	A	19.	C
10.	A	20.	C

21. D
22. C
23. B
24. A
25. B

TEST 2

DIRECTIONS: Each question or incomplete statement is followed by several suggested answers or completions. Select the one that BEST answers the question or completes the statement. PRINT THE LETTER OF THE CORRECT ANSWER IN THE SPACE AT THE RIGHT.

1. When shampooing lightened hair, use

    A. a mild shampoo and tepid water
    B. hot water
    C. liquid dry shampoo
    D. strong shampoo

    1.____

2. When pressing hair over a loose scalp, use

    A. large sections   B. more oil
    C. small sections   D. more pressure

    2.____

3. The EASIEST type of hair to press is _____ hair.

    A. coarse   B. wiry
    C. fine   D. gray

    3.____

4. The PROPER position to hold a strand of hair while it is being wound is to hold it

    A. in a downward position
    B. to one side
    C. up and out from the scalp
    D. in a slanting position

    4.____

5. Cold wave curls are wrapped without tension to

    A. give a loose wave
    B. give a tight wave
    C. allow the hair to contract
    D. prevent overprocessing

    5.____

6. The neutralizing time in cold permanent waving is comparable to one of the following in heat permanent waving:

    A. steaming time   B. cooling time
    C. wrapping time   D. test curl time

    6.____

7. In giving a cold wave to tinted hair, you must expect

    A. the true hair shade to appear   B. some discoloration
    C. the hair to become darker   D. some hair breakage

    7.____

8. Cold wave solution applied to the scalp may cause scalp

    A. discoloration   B. irritation   C. tension   D. wens

    8.____

9. End papers used in winding hair ends for a cold permanent wave must be

    A. non-porous   B. moisture proof
    C. porous   D. dampened with a fixative

    9.____

10. If tension is used in winding the hair, the action of the cold wave solution may be

    A. retarded
    B. accelerated
    C. stopped entirely
    D. neutralized

    10.____

11. The deciding factor in determining the processing time in cold permanent waving is the hair

    A. texture B. pigment C. porosity D. density

    11.____

12. Sectioning and winding the hair for a cold permanent wave usually begins at the _____ area.

    A. crown
    B. frontal
    C. nape
    D. temple

    12.____

13. Before starting a cold permanent wave, the hair should be shampooed and thoroughly

    A. lubricated
    B. saturated
    C. rinsed
    D. neutralized

    13.____

14. A cosmetology license issued by the division of licenses is *not* needed for an operator who gives only

    A. shampoos
    B. scalp treatments
    C. manicures
    D. facials

    14.____

15. The texture of hair that requires the LONGEST processing time in cold permanent waving is _____ hair.

    A. fine B. wiry C. bleached D. dyed

    15.____

16. A preparation used in beauty culture that is *highly* inflammable is

    A. brilliantine
    B. astringent
    C. hair lacquer
    D. cold-wave lotion

    16.____

17. A bluing rinse may be given

    A. to tone down over-hennaed hair
    B. to give a platinum shade to bleached hair
    C. to take the yellow out of gray or white hair
    D. for all the above purposes

    17.____

18. Upon entering a beauty shop, you find that the operator, in preparation for a patron, has assembled, gauze, orris powder, shaker, hair tonic, cotton, hair brush. You would surmise that the preparation is for a

    A. scalp treatment for oily hair
    B. scalp treatment for dry hair
    C. pre-shampoo treatment
    D. dry shampoo

    18.____

19. Comb pressing is known as a _____ press.

    A. regular B. marcel C. hard D. soft

    19.____

20. A substance that is NOT present in hair is 20.____

    A. carbon   B. hydrogen   C. nitrogen   D. kaoline

21. Of the following, the MOST recent development in correcting broken and bitten nails is the application of 21.____

    A. "Nail Fix"   B. "Patti Nails"
    C. artificial nails   D. Revlon's "Lactol"

22. Electrolysis permanently removes hair by destroying the hair 22.____

    A. shaft   B. root   C. bulb   D. papilla

23. The purpose of the neutralizer in the cold-wave process is to 23.____

    A. fix the curl   B. expand the hair
    C. soften the hair   D. remove the oil from the hair

24. Which of the following statements is INCORRECT? 24.____

    A. A knowledge of hair porosity is important to a beauty operator who does hair tinting.
    B. The ends of the hair take tint slower than the rest of the hair
    C. 28% ammonia water is used in some bleaching mixtures.
    D. Powdered magnesium carbonate is sometimes used when bleaching hair with hydrogen peroxide and ammonia water.

25. Which of the following statements is INCORRECT? 25.____

    A. Metallic hair tints are recommended by professional beauticians.
    B. It is sometimes necessary to pre-soften hair in giving a hair tint.
    C. A beautician should know when it is advisable to use a hair filler
    D. Under proper conditions bleached hair can usually be given a successful permanent wave.

KEY (CORRECT ANSWERS)

1. A
2. C
3. A
4. D
5. C

6. B
7. B
8. B
9. C
10. A

11. A
12. C
13. B
14. C
15. B

16. C
17. D
18. D
19. D
20. D

21. B
22. D
23. A
24. B
25. A

www.ingramcontent.com/pod-product-compliance
Lightning Source LLC
Chambersburg PA
CBHW081827300426
44116CB00014B/2505